REVERENCE
FOR THE SOUL

REVERENCE FOR THE SOUL

Richard Schain

ISBN #:   Softcover   1-4010-0435-0

This book was printed in the United States of America.

To order additional copies of this book, contact:
Xlibris Corporation
1-888-795-4274
www.Xlibris.com
Orders@Xlibris.com

CONTENTS

TO MELANIE – MY DANCING STAR

.

PREFACE

You will discover in this book someone working at an arduous task. He appears to be obsessed with it. One might consider his situation analogous to a sculptor working on a piece of recalcitrant stone. Chip, chip here, chip, chip there, now back to an area hammered out before, then to the back of the stone, then to the front. All the while, he is industriously trying to bring out the figure he perceives in the rough, resistant rock. It is a difficult labor.

But what exactly is the task that this person has undertaken and what kind of stone is he working upon? Shall we take his words at face value and accept the statement that his task is to "form his soul?" Shall we accept that all the repetitions, proclamations, confessions and justifications within the writing bear witness to the unforthcoming nature of the substance of which the writer is composed?

Now one might say with justification that even if a metaphor such as "formation of the soul" were to be taken seriously (certainly not by scientific psychologists), is it not presumptuous of someone to expend so much energy and so much time on his own nebulous self? Are there not many larger problems and more important issues in the world at large? There is not even the distraction of a story to help a reader maintain his interest in the often siege-engine-like style with which the writer attacks his stone.

What can be said to such objections? In truth, nothing of consequence because the nature of a writer's writings and a reader's interests are not to be altered by prefaces. The writer has done his work, he has gathered strength and mastered his medium as the writing proceeds. Whether it will be of interest to others is a matter not easily ascertained. A few observations, however, may be made.

The writer is doing in this work what he considers to be the most important task of his existence; the delineation and establishment of what he calls his soul. It is no exaggeration to say that he feels his principal mission in life lies in the fulfillment of this task. He is not interested in the world at large or the problems of its society except insofar as they pertain to his mission. In the words of Kierkegaard, "Whatever I do, I do *proprio marte, propriis auspiciis, proprio stipendi*, in short as a proprietor." Dispensing with the Latin: on my own initiative, for my own purposes, and with my own resources. The reader whose expectations are not congruent with this point of view should go elsewhere for his reading.

Sometimes, however, an apology–in the antique sense of the word–may have some place in a writing. After all, against all odds, this book may enter into circulation and thus be in need of readers. And who knows? Perhaps all the knotty problems of the society at large are best approached via the microcosmic world of the individual.

Therefore, I will say that the central theme of the writing, the subject most discussed, the object of all the citations, the *value* most firmly asserted, is that of the primacy of individual thought in the human condition. Not thought for instrumental purposes in order to feather one's nest but thought as a goal to be sought after for its own value. Thought is conceived of as ultimately identical with the metaphysical concept of "soul" because it is within the ramifications and relationships of thought that the soul is formed. The title of the work underlines this theme; reverence for soul means reverence for thought which is the proper state of mind for man as *Homo sapiens*. The writer focuses on his own soul because this is what he knows best and what is his responsibility. Others will have their own responsibilities to assume.

The writer has done his work; a reader need only consider whether reading this book relates to his own work. For in the end, doing one's own work is the only subject truly deserving of attention. It is in the identification of the work to be done that the difficulty lies. But this is a topic deserving of a book in itself. This preface is best terminated by a passage from the writing itself:

"My life is like a river flowing somewhere even if I often have difficulty in determining the direction of flow. Yet there is no doubt in my mind that it after something. As I look back on its turns and twists, its sudden changes of direction, its accelerations and periods of stagnation, I am struck by the relentless flow. It is going somewhere. I can honestly say that all my life, I have been seeking to develop the interior consciousness that I call my soul. All the experiences, all the reading, studying, writing, all the pursuits of evanescent insights have been exercises in the development of my consciousness. I do not say there is anything necessarily admirable in such a life, it is merely the life I have been compelled to live. As Thoreau said, I respect my aspirations if not always my activities. Development of my mind has always been my aspiration, and, always, if I have been too long diverted from this goal, I have found ways to return to it."

Sonoma County, California
October 1999

PRELUDE

Things don't work. That's the main point of everything, things don't work. I've been a good citizen most of my life but things haven't worked. My eyes have slowly opened to the knowledge that things haven't worked. I've followed all the rules, done all the right things, met all the right people, gotten the right education, married the right woman, had the right children, live in the right home, make the right amount of money–but things still don't work. It's a heart-rending experience. I'm totally at sea and don't know where to turn. Something is rotten here; I'd like to clean out everything, decontaminate the world, kick all the liars out.

Through my mind's eye, the universe has become a grotesque nightmare, an expressionist horror story. Everything is red and purple, bleached bones lie all around me, people have dripping fangs, blood is leaking from a thousand open sores of contorted figures surrounding me. What does it all mean? Why is it all here? Where is it all going? I'm like an abandoned child, lost in a dark wood of misery and ignorance. Something terrible has been done to me, I've been poisoned by some noxious substance in my upbringing. People are lying to me all the time. I've got to get out of this place. But where can I go?

I can't ever allow myself to forget how much I've been lied to. There must be something illegal about lying to people, especially to children. You can't lie to a woman about marriage, you get brought up on breach of promise. How much worse it is to lie to a child, making him believe he will be happy if he lives his life a certain way. I must try to straighten myself out. I must find the truth.

* * *

PART I— STONEWORK

> "Our thoughts are the epochs in our lives; all else is but as a journal of the winds that blew while we were here."
>
> Henry David Thoreau

My literary isolation has been complete for a number of years. Not one of my published works has been discussed in any literary review other than a notice of appearance. This after some ten years of a steady prose output. The hundred readers that Henry Miller said was sufficient to justify authorship does not come close to existing in my case. An objective observer would judge my writing career to be an abject failure.

Nevertheless, I write. The desire has increased in intensity through the years. There is something that drives me on which has nothing to do with the acknowledged purposes of the activity. It is a personal affair, something involved with the very fiber of my being; my soul so to speak. The fact is that the more I write, the more I realize the motivation has little to do with being read by others. The moment I hear the word "market," I shy away like a frightened deer and give no further attention. I refuse to have anything to do with writers' conferences, courses, seminars, workshops and all the other euphemisms by which successful writers derive monies from unsuccessful ones.

What would I do with literary recognition?–it would only awaken the latent feelings of contempt and aversion that I have for all the institutions which I have experienced and would inflict upon me the loss of intimacy and privacy that such recognition entails.

It is important for me to understand the meaning which writing has in my life because I am not one to be driven by blind passions, literary or otherwise. I have thought
all this before but I need to think it through over and over again. The only way I have found to become known to myself is through writing.

* * *

How much mental effort, how much anxiety, how many wrong directions have been required for me to grasp the primacy of my own soul over my surroundings! How often do I still look to the outside when I should be looking within. My education has been totally lacking in instruction about the nature of my own interior reality; consequently, it is almost instinctive for me to look to some kind of exterior structure or community for obtaining meaning in my life. Like a dog who runs for the rubber bone no matter how often he finds it to be inedible, so it is when society gives me a nod of approval, my instincts are to rise on my haunches and come to pleasurable attention.

Last week I happened to notice my name mentioned in an obscure professional publication dealing with a topic to which I had devoted far too much of my energies during my mental childhood. I know the subject to be of little importance and the controversy surrounding it to be trivial, elaborated largely to advance the careers of academicians. Still, the mention of my name in a professional publication is capable of producing a shiver of pleasure within me. I realize that my efforts at freeing myself from the prison of professional vanity have not yet been successful. At such times, I am impatient with myself because I seem incapable of overcoming childish desires for recognition. As long as my vanity is fed whenever I am noticed in world around me, I will never be what I want most to be—a free mind conscious of the nature of its own being and in charge of its external relationships.

What I want of the world is that it know who I am. I am not a creature of a profession nor am I a paterfamilias, an American, a Jew or a male animal. These are all roles that have been assigned to me by society or by nature or a combination of both. But these roles have never done anything for me except to assist with mechanics of survival and procreation. The dues are long since paid and more than paid for that assistance. I am even willing to continue to pay much as I pay for my insurance policy, professional society or taxes to the government. But I am no more any one of these societal roles than I am a "Taxpayer" as I am referred to in the governmental forms sent to me annually. "I am I" as God says of himself in Scriptures and I would like all to know that this refers to me also.

* * *

Sitting on the benches in Sproul Plaza, I observed a young man, shirtless and in shorts, posting notices on a student bulletin board. He was posting many copies of the same notice everywhere, covering other notices so that only his could be read. It proclaimed in giant black print: DEMONSTRATE FOR THE PEOPLE OF EL SALVADOR, and gave details of the demonstration to be held on the following week. The posters it covered over were of a similar nature, announcing other demonstrations, classes, lectures, performances—the usual events that go on in the circuses of Berkeley. No doubt this notice was soon to be covered over by others in the anarchical struggle for vertical space in the area.

I have never discovered a cause not personally affecting me that I consider to be worth my energy. One may attribute this to selfishness on my part but I perceive it as lack of conviction of my ability to see the truth in external situations. What do I know of conditions in El Salvador?–or in Nicaragua or South Africa or Palestine? I do not have the slightest inkling of what the people there feel and think or what the truth is of their circumstances. Nor do I have any idea of how my government should behave toward their governments or to the multitude of factions that seek power in them. When I was young, I fervently believed that the Communist Party represented the struggling masses abroad and that my government had erred in opposing it. I know now that opinion was grievously incorrect. During World War II, the Japanese were portrayed to me as evil little men intent on destroying my country but I now know that I knew nothing of the facts of the situation. When the Vietnam war occurred, I was persuaded that the destiny of the Vietnamese people lay with their indigenous leaders but I no longer believe that the people of South Vietnam have been benefited by the hegemony of the rulers of North Vietnam. Today, I am assailed by proponents of endless causes, all of which are represented to me as moral issues. But I am no longer so naive as to think I can make judgments about causes exterior to my own individuality.

* * *

I live in a society animated by external affairs. It is only in groups that people come alive, it is only as members of communities that individuals find the courage to assert themselves. Affirmative action applies only to the individual as a member of some community, never to himself as an individual independent of a community.

Every community I have ever belonged to diminished me. Membership in a community is an adaptation to the material elements of life at the expense of the individual–the *soul* of the individual which, as I have said, no one believes in any longer. Even in the arts, in which individuality is the *sine qua non* of meaningful activity, one finds an increasing importance of "community" in which the artist locates his sense of personal identity.

My alienation is a source of pride to me when I truly consider the condition of my society. Painful and disappointing as it is at times to lack any feeling of social support for myself as a writer, I prefer this isolation to the false security of the institutionalized writer in the commercial world, in academia, in the trade guilds of literary America. My isolation renders me clear-eyed, I see the reality of things, I am forced to rely on myself instead of succumbing to the temptations of communal idolatry and phoniness. The dog who is forced to forage for himself instead of begging for table scraps has a better sense of the realities of life than does a domestic pet. So it is with the writer who must forage for himself amidst the pressures of the "communities" around him.

* * *

It is not enough to be lucid in this life, one must also have values. Christianity triumphed over the pagan world not because of greater lucidity–it could never hope to match the lucidity of the Greek philosophers–but because of its more highly developed values. Repeatedly I have noticed that if my sense of values does not keep up with my lucidity, my thinking mechanism begins to fail like a vehicle running out of fuel. It is necessary for me to *value* as well as to see. It is my opinion that many great independent personalities suffered a deterioration of their personalities from lack of values to match their lucidity. It has been said that committed Christians are "metaphysically happy" because of their powerful value system. What Christianity introduced of importance into the world was a well-defined system of spiritual values that provided spiritual sustenance to the Christian world.

Nevertheless, violation of the intellectual conscience by Christian doctrine is slowly but steadily resulting in a breaking down of religious faith among Christians, consequently the spiritual value system of Christianity is breaking down also.

* * *

I am not apologetic about the amount of time I spend thinking by myself. It is hard for me to recall any waking hours alone when I am not thinking about imperative questions. For me, thinking is living the kind of life I wish to live. Some say that genuine living is to love another person but it seems to me this is just another device to escape one's duty to oneself.

The only place in my home where I can really think is seated with my notebook or at my typewriter. Otherwise, I am assailed by reminders of things outside of myself that clamor for attention. Even when there are no household chores to be done, no correspondence to be attended to, no books to be browsed through or programs to be watched on the tube, the mere presence of a surrounding physical world to which I am connected in a proprietary manner disturbs the workings of my consciousness. It is necessary for me to depart from my house or sit secluded in my writing area in order to be really able to attend to my interior world.

Over the years, it is this interior world which has become the real world for me. I still participate in the society, such as it is, which surrounds me; I hold a job, converse with fellow-workers, neighbors and acquaintances, participate in those activities which are necessary for me to maintain my position as an independent citizen with my own shelter and sustenance. But all this has become more and more unreal to me. At times, I fear that the mental discipline that maintains me in society may not compensate for the interior withdrawal. So far, this has not happened. However, most of my energies and desires are invested in the world of my interior consciousness which is the principal focus of reality for me.

Although it is possible to argue about the nature of reality and to discuss at length the uncertainties of an exterior world recognized only through the senses versus an interior world of thought known through a mysterious consciousness, the preference of an individual for one or another of these worlds is not a matter of logic, it is a matter of personal inclination. One could argue equally well in favor of materialism or idealism (in the Platonic sense) and ultimately one has to concede both approaches to the human condition have valid claims to reality. However, an individual seems to be psychologically incapable of maintaining an unbiased attitude toward these two positions; sooner or later, one of them becomes the favored attitude. One cannot, in truth, serve both God and Mammon, purity of heart is indeed to wish one thing, thus it finally turns out that monism is not a philosophical posture, it is a psychological imperative. The Roman Catholic Church's expectations of its clergy derive from its superior psychological insight into the human condition.

In the heart of my consciousness, which is the only place that counts in a developed person, I am a recluse because materialism as a way of life is unfulfilling and belief in the Judeo-Christian God is too offensive to my intellectual conscience. Confronted with a choice between boredom and dishonesty, I have opted for the reclusive state. Let the materialists have their possessions, careers and families, let the religionists prate about their God who loves them; I want nothing to do with either of these states of mind. In the solitude of my interior being, I have discovered satisfactions far surpassing those of the inanities going on all around me.

* * *

Interior consciousness is not something that appears in an individual overnight. I have never met a child possessing what I consider to be a genuine interior consciousness. Children may have emotions, feelings, desires–but not the essential ingredient of a higher consciousness that is *the augmentation of being* produced by thought. It is perhaps not profitable to engage in excess semantic discussion, but I believe it is proper to regard the being of interior consciousness as identical with the *soul*, a term which is familiar to most civilized societies. As I see it, it is absurd to regard children as possessing souls. In my own case, I cannot remember an interior consciousness, i.e., a soul, until I was approaching puberty. There is no reason for considering all of the stimulus-response behaviors of childhood as indicative of a soul; they are nothing but the mental and physical gymnastics of little monkeys possessed of memories. To have a soul means to be conscious of the diverse levels of being of the universe in relation to the self and all the nuances of feelings associated with such consciousness. Such a state of being is part of the mind of children only in exceptional cases.

The essential aspect of a soul is its non-materiality. Modern science does not accept this concept; the most ridiculous assertions have been made by scientists that think themselves able to define consciousness and the soul in materialist terms. Inevitably, the soul is relegated to the sphere of mysticism or "epiphenomena" i.e., non-being. But the interior consciousness is no more susceptible to materialist analysis than is the beginning of time or the limits of the cosmos. It is enough that we are capable of interior consciousness and possess the energies to promote its development.

How does one become conscious of himself as a spiritual, i.e., soul-containing being? Certainly not through education or conversation or all the myriad activities by which one insures his place in society. Nor can anyone apprehend the soul by reading books no matter how authoritative they may be. Consciousness is a *miraculous* phenomenon emerging in human beings as a consequence of the human condition and its experiences. One may lose a spouse, a child, even a whole family, thereby experiencing the most painful state of deprivation and grief but the soul makes its appearance only when consciousness emerges as an interior state distinct from painful emotion. So it is with all experiences which may or may not be productive of greater consciousness.

Culture, in its ideal form, is the expression of a shared consciousness of being. But no parent, teacher, friend, book or artwork can instill consciousness into a person; they can only bring out the latent consciousness already present. There are few experiences more ennobling than a sharing of consciousness, no debt greater than that owed to the one who has helped an individual bring his latent consciousness into full view.

* * *

The society within which I live has done little to assist me to develop a consciousness of being. Like Thoreau, I can honestly say that I have never learned anything from my elders with regard to this question which is *the* question of the human condition. Of course, I cannot deny that I have learned a great deal about the mechanics of living, techniques for survival, instruction in a profession and so forth. But nothing about the question of being. This is why I am a recluse and why I turned to writing for the development of my soul. When I was younger, I was unsure what I was looking for but in time it became clear to me; I was looking to form my soul. I consider no activity to be more important.

I can now see, living as I do in the most materialist society known to history, that there was little reason to think anyone would or could help me to develop my soul. The religions of my society are largely superannuated relics of former civilizations. Rousseau has put in the mouth of his Savoyard Vicar everything necessary to say about western religions; there is nothing more to be added (though I do not agree with Rousseau in many of his other thoughts about spiritual matters). How any thinking person can take the western monotheisms seriously as a means to increased consciousness of being is beyond my comprehension. What I aspire toward is knowledge of reality, not tales for children or commemoration of family traditions. Moralizing homilies do not produce or substitute for interior development. Having had no personal connection with the founders of western religions (or any other religions), and having no experiences consistent with their assertions, dogmatic traditions and teachings are for me merely meaningless jabber.

What is significant to me is the awareness of my own soul and my contact with the souls of others, derived largely through the written word. These contacts have helped me crystallize my own thoughts. I once read a line in Lautréamont to the effect that he had never encountered a soul similar to his own. I cannot conceive of sustaining existence with such a thought. To never encounter at any level of being a soul that resembles one's own is an admission of extreme personal deviancy or grotesqueness of being. It is necessary to feel that one resembles others in the human race; otherwise, one is a teratological monstrosity that will be eliminated by nature.

When I come in contact with a thought of another person that produces the sensation of kinship, my isolation is relieved, I feel that I am part of humanity, be the connection ever so tenuous. It is this experience which has kept me from total spiritual reclusiveness, allowing me to identify with humanity if not the culture of my own society.

* * *

My "métier" is that of a physician, a fact that may surprise a reader of this writing. I hate all métiers but fortunately for my survival in this world, I did not come to this realization until middle age, consistent with my overall slowness of development. My connection with society is almost entirely through this métier which accounts for my state of spiritual reclusiveness. My family ties also connect me to some degree with society but these are slight, based as they are almost entirely upon sentiment. I have never been one to derive much gratification from sentimental ties.

I have not mentioned love, more specifically erotic love, which has been a most powerful force in my life. For many years, it was the sole factor that kept me from being a total hermit. Were it not for the erotic impulse, I probably would have long since retreated to a mountain top. Nevertheless, one cannot live for erotic love alone, and I have been forced to come to terms with my existence beyond erotic relationships.

It is a great error to seek fulfillment in life exclusively through society, no matter whether it be hedonistic gratifications, success in a career, or relationships with another person or persons. All of these come down ultimately to the physical dimensions of life no matter how idealized one tries to make these activities. The soul is not fed through social activities, it is fed through the development of consciousness. Possessions, careers, relationship–these are all distractions which are of value only insofar as they provide experiences upon which consciousness develops. The hunger for experience is the underlying common human denominator. Of course, as an animal that needs to breathe, eat, copulate, one must have his private areas of satisfaction. There is no point, however, in exaggerating their significance.

As a professional person, providing services for which I am paid, I understand fully what is expected of me. Technical proficiency–plus a few drops of human kindness to make the medicines more palatable–this is what I provide. What an absurdity to imagine that this kind of activity could ever satisfy the needs of my soul. Yet I am surrounded by people who think that their professional success has fulfilled their need for self-development. Add to this a household with growing children plus a suburban home with all the amenities and they think they are God's chosen creatures. To me, they are no more human than the apes I see confined in the San Francisco zoo. I desire to have nothing to do with such ignorant creatures. I far prefer to read Thoreau or improve my Greek. Living souls in dead books are infinitely superior to dead souls in living bodies.

* * *

I consider the principal responsibility of an able-minded person is to establish his independence. Early in life, this requires becoming mobile and acquiring spoken language. Gradually a young person emancipates himself from his family and immediate surroundings. Acquiring a trade and a knowledge of society are essential ingredients for establishing independence. When a person reaches the adult stage in life, has succeeded in gaining his livelihood, has established his own household and style of living, he is regarded as an independent being and becomes an accepted member of his society. Social approval is his reward his efforts in establishing an independent position for himself.

A

But at a deeper level, independent material existence is only the beginning for a human being who wishes to be really independent. He must learn to emancipate himself from society just as he emancipated himself from his family. The independence that has real significance is spiritual independence in which the individual no longer relies on society to solve the basic *problem of existence* for him. Society only provides roles for individuals, it does not solve their problem of existence. There has not been a single role assigned to me by my society that created a sense of wellbeing in me. There is no role that can create wellbeing except that of an independent human being, a *Homo sapiens* which means development of an interior consciousness. The Delphic prescription for happiness was *gnothi seauton*–know thyself; no better formulation of the problem of existence has ever been offered. Whenever I rely upon a role to solve the problem of my existence, I fall into a state of anxious depression, an *Angst* from which I can only emerge by shedding the role, not only in a concrete manner but also psychologically, so that it has only superficial significance and can be easily discarded.

* * *

It has been said that the desire for fame is the last problem to be confronted by the one searching for wisdom. The love of money, sex, property, offspring–all these can be sooner or later put in perspective by an intelligent individual. But the desire to be highly regarded in one's society tenaciously clings to the individual in spite of all his efforts to be free of it. What Rousseau said of the philosophers of his day–that they one and all would prefer some knowledge they had gained be never known if others were the ones to gain renown for its discovery–applies to most people whatever their position in society. Whereas adults usually emancipate themselves from the need for parental or family approval (not always, however), it is rare to find an individual who does not rely on societal endorsement for his feeling of success in life–or if he does not, has not achieved this feeling by a retreat into misanthropy. Social bondage or misanthropy often appear to be the only alternatives with respect to dependence on societal approval.

While it is generally accepted that it is inappropriate for a person to remain dependent upon his family, it is not at all recognized that it is inappropriate for a person to remain psychologically dependent upon his society. But why should one condition be more acceptable than the other? Why should it be shameful for a grown person to be uncertain in his actions without the consent of a parent whereas there is no stigma at all applied if he is unable to act without societal approval. Conversely, when the myriad of celebrities spawned by society unabashedly bask in societal adulation, they are not regarded as infantile creatures as they would if they were reacting to parental approval; rather it is thought they are enjoying the fruits of success and their position is admired, if not envied.

Celebrity status for a person is a shameful condition, branding him as a creature symbiotically fused to his society instead of emancipated from it. Just as a dysfunctional society seeks out persons to imprison in celebrity status, so dysfunctional individuals seek out this status from society. The only celebrity status that is proper is the posthumous one when it no longer has an impact on the living individual, an impact which is necessarily destructive to the inner self.

I do not think there is much chance for widespread human development in any culture which has not come to grips with the significance of fame and celebrity status. As long as persons seek to solve the problem of existence through societal adulation, they will never develop the interior consciousness that marks the developed human being. The inclination of the ancient Greek *polis* to expel the celebrity from the confines of the city has a practical basis which has been unduly criticized. Celebrities are dangerous models for the young. Like some contagious illness, the taste for fame easily spreads throughout a society and becomes embedded in its fabric. Until the consciousness of fame as a wrong direction in life becomes part of the culture of a society, it is impossible to direct individuals within that culture toward interior growth.

* * *

Fame within a society is an obstacle to the development of the self; consequently, insofar as literary expression is a manifestation of the self, fame is an obstacle to literary expression. Intermittently, I have longings for the rewards of fame, the pleasures of being recognized and sought out by others, the warm feeling of having an established place in society. But then I think of the sacrifices that would be entailed; the loss of my precious anonymity, my privacy, the intimate relationship I have with my work. What would be the good of multiplying my social contacts when I have so little common ground with almost everyone I meet. My spirit thrives in solitude; transplanted into an alien climate, it would wither or ossify. I have been fortunate in being permitted to develop without public exposure.

I remember the oft-repeated comment of Nicolai Berdyaev that "belief in God is one's charter of liberty." Without a belief in God, Berdyaev asserts, the individual cannot escape being overpowered by the demonic forces of society. Berdyaev, who was one of the few really original thinkers of our century, advocated Christianity as the vehicle for belief in God. What I learned from Berdyaev—or rather was reminded by him of what experience had already taught me—is that without a *metaphysical awareness*, it is impossible to escape being overwhelmed by society. Whether it be through race, revolution or organized religion, through profession or nationality, through family or property, sooner or later the object world tricks the individual into the abdication of the interior self. Without this awareness, the individual is a helpless pawn of the societal forces enveloping him. How can the speck of sand called a human being, immersed as it is in the oceans of time and space, maintain its freedom when confronted with the material force of external nature and society. It is a hopeless idea; the leaders of society are well advised to rely on behavior training rather than personal responsibility to incorporate humans into social networks. But when one expands the interior self, when "being" takes precedence over "doing," the individual then possesses a bulwark of freedom grounded in reality instead of illusion. The soul of the individual is, in fact, the principal reality for *Homo sapiens*–all external realities are technical problems of physical survival that, without an inner reality, have little meaning for the individual.

* * *

More and more, it is becoming clear to me that my reclusive state is necessary, not out of distaste of society, but out of the need for self-protection. One does not mingle freely in leper colonies unless there is a very good reason. My life is healthier when I avoid society; every time I allow myself to unguardedly enter into it, the old noxious habits return, I become again dependent, I again feel the need for external approval, my internal self becomes less real as the outside world impinges upon and smothers it. It might appear that as one grows older, one would become more self-sufficient mentally but my society works in an opposite direction, it attempts to make the individual more dependent upon it.

Awarding achievement prizes to individuals is like inviting them to enter opium dens (or however one becomes habituated to drugs in the present age).

* * *

Perhaps there is some grand design at work in the population explosion that has afflicted planet Earth. As the numbers of people ascend into the billions, there is less and less space for the individual to develop himself; more and more one resembles an ant in gigantic societal anthills; the interior world becomes progressively more difficult to sustain. Nowhere is this clearer than in the world of literature in which huge publishing houses oriented toward gigantic readerships dominate the activities of the writer. The interior self is an object of derision and ridicule, the "market" is the only reality for publishers operating multimillion dollar enterprises. But it is the same with everything; societies are becoming so intricately developed that the requirement of social interactions overshadow and destroy the soul. The individual who has not discovered his interior self–more importantly, has not *valued* his interior self above the exterior world–is doomed to degrading anthill existence no matter how much it is glorified with societal clichés.

It is easy to determine the motivation behind one's activities–one merely has to observe how he expects to be rewarded for them. If the rewards involve money, relationships or societal attentions, than the activity is not motivated toward development of the interior self.

* * *

Sexuality links one to the outer world; it is not necessary to forge any other bonds to become a prisoner of society.

* * *

I recently had occasion to converse at length with a professional colleague; an individual with some distinction in his career. For him, there is a reality to his work that appears to be adequate to his needs as a human being. He seems to be "metaphysically content" with his life. He has made his decision about the nature of reality, it is present in the life that he leads which is centered on the study of certain obscure medical disorders.

The discovery of reality requires a judgement as to where it is to be found. My first philosophical writing was entitled *Affirmations of Reality* where I attempted to discuss this issue. In the opinion of my medical colleague, the real world is the object world surrounding him and he participates in reality to the extent that he is involved in the object world. This is the common opinion of the man on the street. The other day I read an interview with Pierre Cardin, one of the most "successful" individuals in France today. He was sufficiently able to abstract from his work to propose that his success was based on his "love of objects" and his emotional investment in them. His decision about the nature of reality has certainly brought him success by modern standards. For the average person, reality is the circumstances in which they live; when they are able to adapt to these circumstances, they regard themselves as living in reality.

It may be, however, that there are many realities, and that the reality to be found in the surrounding object world is an inferior one to that of one's own soul. The reality I cherish exists in my own state of consciousness. The capacity for participating in this reality is directly related to the degree to which one is able to overcome the exterior world and direct attention inward. The greatest pleasures come from enhancing consciousness, the most grinding boredom and discontent come from being chained to the object world. I know of no greater defeat than being forced to direct all one's vital energies into the exterior circumstances of his life. It seems to me that such a state of affairs is a total denial of the human condition which demands that the individual develop the consciousness within himself.

* * *

Christianity is a continuing enigma to me. I constantly try to distinguish between the Christian phenomenon which is a spiritual orientation and Christian institutions which are in no essential way different from other social or political institutions. The latter are of little interest to me. But the spiritual orientation of Christian belief is more related to the real world I perceive than is any other belief system with which I am familiar. The Christian is oriented toward his soul more as a result of his tradition rather than his personal effort. Whereas I have found my interior self through intense thought, the Christian claims to find this self by means of the grace of his God. In fact, I am not very impressed with the spirituality of the professed Christians I meet in daily life. They seem to have formulas rather than interior realities. They have solved the problem of existence through deference to higher authorities; I do not care for such a solution that appears to me to be a suppression of the problem rather than its resolution. I have to reconquer the problem of existence every day; perhaps my way does not lead to tranquillity but it leaves me an independent being with a sense of my task in life.

"By their fruits ye shall know them," it says in the Gospels. What is to be said about the contemporary charismatic preachers who represent the fruit of Christianity? I have recently been watching one of them broadcast daily on a television channel. His venality is overwhelming, it appears that the sole criterion of Christian faith is the size of the donation to the preacher's organization. This character certainly puts on a good show; my main objection to him is the contradictory nature of his situation—one cannot serve both God and mammon.

The individual who is so confident of his own wisdom that he gives absolute direction to others is not an individual worthy of much trust. Every honest person—priest, professor or otherwise—knows that his own position is so uncertain that he has very little energies left over for genuine assistance to others. He may act confident but it is a sham. Whenever I see someone, no matter what his walk in life, derive his personal fulfillment from directing others, I feel that he has lost his integrity and is not to be relied upon. He is not developing his interior self, he is rather involved with the external world of objects whether they be dead or living. It is quite revealing that the psychoanalytic term for human relationships is "object relationships."

The objection to the Judeo-Christian ethic is its misleading emphasis. There is nothing wrong in helping or loving others—these relationships provide consolations in a cruel society—it is that this is not the main task of an individual and does not help him get at the problem of his own existence.

"Others" are the outside world no matter how one romanticizes relationships or subjects them to ethical judgments. It is foolishness to imagine that virtue is acquired if one loves others as oneself; such a thought ignores the real issue. It is not a matter of loving the self, it is a matter of *creating* the self which does not come about through external relationships regardless of moralistic intentions. Anyone who really takes his own soul seriously, who has reverence for what is within himself, cannot believe that it is enhanced through concentrating on others. Nietzsche perceived that guiding others spiritually was a kind of egotistical power play irrespective of fancy phrases that justify it.

There is no reality for a person which approaches the reality of the interior self–deluding oneself into thinking otherwise forfeits the chance for creating one's own soul. How can one believe that the pious pastor shepherding his flock through the world is doing anything for his own interior being? Or that the zealous preacher expending his energies to galvanize his audience is making himself into a better human being? I do not believe it. If there is any wisdom in Christian institutions, it is to be found in the monasteries and convents, not in the churches or the ministry.

* * *

I don't mind the word "culture." It is when I hear the word "market" that I wish I had a revolver to reach for. This term produces a visceral reaction in me as though I had ingested some foul or putrefying substance that I should regurgitate as soon as possible. Whereas I can forgive politicians, doctors and lawyers their posturing as benefactors of the people, I cannot find in myself similar forgiveness for literary persons who should know better. I only see in them new manifestations of the insatiable human need to prey upon the weaknesses of his fellow man. The priests of Christianity are giving way to the priests of literature. But it is the same parasitic relationship; the power hunger of the few feeds upon the dependency of the many. Heraclitus had it wrong, *oi oligoi* are no better than *oi polloi*, both may represent the tendency of a society toward degeneracy.

For me, there is a spiritual quality to the writer-reader relationship. The interior self of the one is communicated to the interior self of the other. Out of this contact arises an enhanced awareness of self as something more than mere biology. When the writer, by orienting to the concept of "market," sabotages this relationship, he destroys the literary experience as a means for self-development. The professional writer is the death of literature as one of the ways in which the soul evolves.

Literature should have a sacred quality. Human beings need to have a sense of sacredness which only means that certain things have more value than others. The measure of sacredness is reality; that which has a greater portion of reality is more sacred than that which has a lesser. For *Homo sapiens*, his interior consciousness, his soul, is the most real thing he will ever experience, consequently, it is what most deserves to be treated as sacred. Whatever elevates his consciousness shares in this sacredness. If he does not have reverence for his soul as something sacred, however, he is bound to find some lesser reality outside of himself that will be the object of his worship.

* * *

The emptiness of many devout Christians does not surprise me. The worst aberration of the Christian mentality is to foster the idea that relationships with others are more important than the development of the self. The grossest materialist is preferable to the pious Christian because the former has the possibility of redirecting his efforts while the latter is usually hopelessly ensnared in the delusions of Christian dogma. When one penetrates Christian consciousness and tries to move beyond the peculiar belief in a God who loves him (not to speak of the bizarre notion of a personal savior), one comes upon a great emptiness. The self has not developed, there is a void where consciousness of being should be established. It is like penetrating into the interior of an architecturally magnificent castle in which there are no furnishings. All the devout Christian can find for sustenance is intensifying his bondage to the Christian concept. Fernando Pessoa has a more painful metaphor comparing the Christian phenomenon to a devastating tempest in which the extent of the destruction will not be evident until it has passed.

* * *

Having brought Pessoa to mind, a few remarks about him are in order. As a prose writer, he is the most interesting literary figure of the twentieth century. He permitted himself the indulgence of *portuguesismo* in much of his writing. I suppose it is relatively harmless to regard oneself as carrying the banner of Portuguese literature, considering its minor impact on the world at large. There are few burdens to be carried with the self-image of being Portuguese. As is the case with most individuals committed to their own minds instead of to literary success, his society kept him at arm's length. During his lifetime, he was left alone to wrestle with the problem of existence. Because in his case, the clash of tradition and individuality was not so heavily weighted on the side of the culture, Pessoa was able to produce a remarkable body of literary work reflecting the inner man.

What does it mean to be an English language writer? Much the same, I imagine, as it was to be a Christian in sixteenth century Spain. The English language culture is so dominant in the world today that its orientations and attitudes seem to be as if Holy Writ, impossible to contradict. It needs to be remembered that the constraints and beliefs of a culture do not necessarily represent the parameters of reality but are only those of a particular culture at a particular stage of development. First and foremost, the materialist worldview is dominant in English language literary activity. The skepticism that is always associated with a materialist worldview determines the orientation of the litterateur for any writing outside vocational, scholarly or traditional religious areas. Widespread absence of belief in the soul (again exempting traditional religion in which it is tolerated for sentimental reasons) causes the English language writer oriented to success to appeal to the standard materialist sensibilities of his audience. In this way, English language literature fits into the most materialist culture known to history.

* * *

The purpose of the writer, just as the purpose of any other artist, just as the purpose of any other human activity, ultimately is reduced to its relationship to the problem of existence. In order for a person to comprehend the meaning of his activities beyond those which are instinctually determined, he must try to comprehend the problem of his existence. What is the *meaning* of the act of writing viewed from the perspective of existence?

It is quite extraordinary to realize how limited and mundane are the prevailing explanations regarding motives for writing. The individual who imagines himself writing for a purpose other than that of monetary rewards finds himself in great difficulties. There are the usual clichés about the need for communication and self expression but what exactly do such phrases mean? In the United States the motive for writing is clear, writers are professionally minded people whose fondest desire is to establish a paid career through writing. When they come to earn a significant income through their writing they soon feel that they would no more write without compensation than any other professional person would without being paid. Uncompensated writing is viewed as a circumstance to be avoided whenever possible. Those writers who do not gain income from writing sooner or later feel they have been rejected by the reading public and give up the effort. Poets, akin to musicians and painters in that they are more inclined to practice their art without remuneration, eventually tend to view their poetizing as an avocation not to be taken too seriously.

Writers almost always come to believe that if they are not noticed by their society, their work is essentially meaningless. Nowhere is this more true than in the United States where the bottom line of being noticed is being paid for services rendered. It is quite pathetic to see how little confidence writers have in themselves who have not received this type of notice. This is because they do not have a consciousness of the relationship of the act of writing to the problem of existence.

This problem of existence for humans has to do with the formation of the self–soul to be more precise–and the act of writing is, as is any other genuinely creative act, intimately related to its formation. If a writer does not regard his soul as an entity grounded in reality but views it as merely a metaphorical phrase not to be taken literally, then he has little basis for relating his writing activity to his own reality or to the problem of his existence. He will not appreciate the essential task of the artist, including the literary artist, of having to progress beyond the mere blind expression of energy in his work to apprehending his own soul and the relationship of his creativity to it.

When I sit with my notebook or typewriter (more recently, "God" forgive me, my "word processor") objectifying my thoughts and feelings, my intuitions, my convictions–something changes within me. The act of exteriorizing what has been interior, of rendering objective what has been subjective, of bringing into the light of day what has been concealed in the darkness of my brain– all this radically changes me as a personality. I am engaged in the act of forming my soul. Writing makes me into something more substantial than I had been before. This transformation of self is what I understand to be the meaning of the creative act.

I sense this increased substantiality in the same way that I know that I exist. It is not true that the best of me is on the printed page, the best of me is the *me* emerging out of my struggle for expression. Others may have access to this me through my writing but even if there are no others, as there well may not be, I exist as something superior to what I was previously. Just as physical effort enlarges muscles that have only existed in incipient form, so creative activity deepens the soul where only the predisposition to a soul existed previously. It must be the same with all art forms, the painter or composer shines forth in the act of painting or composing, he creates his soul. One has only to read the letters of Van Gogh (which I prefer to his paintings) to see the effect his work had upon him.

It is monstrous to say the writer is in the service of his language—as I have read in a speech of a recent Nobel Prize winner in literature—such a statement reveals the absence of a concept of the problem of the existence for the individual, regardless of how talented this Nobelist may be. And it is surely evident that the creative act forming the soul is not a functional of societal approval in any form. God is said by Scripture to have decided on his own that his creation of the world was good, he had no audience. In the same way, the genuinely creative person must be the ultimate arbiter of the value of his creative activity.

* * *

It would be idle for me to pretend that I have not been scarred by my environment. Like most other people, I am habituated to the narcotic of societal approval; it is difficult for me—even at my level of material independence and maturity—to maintain my sense of well being without some stamp of approval analogous to that obtained by inspected cattle or kosher frankfurters. I have yet to develop a fundamental confidence in myself and it is unlikely that I will ever fully do so. This is the result of a faulty upbringing that scarred forever my interior self. Being unable to suppress my intellectual conscience, I have not been able to arrive at societal independence through the route of religious belief as many others have done. Nor has any ideology been able to give the sense of self toward which I aspire. I have never been able to believe that social movements are anything else than the substitution of one group of power brokers for another. Consequently, I have always suffered pangs of discomfort from my isolation in society. I will undoubtedly die suffering such pangs.

Nevertheless, if I cannot feel the way I should, at least I know how I should feel. That is to be independent of ideologies, societies, families and careers. It is my judgment of myself which should be paramount, not that of anyone else–living, dead or yet to be born.

* * *

Discovery of the writings of Fernando Pessoa was a revelation to me–the first new author of real importance that I had come upon in many years. It is worth noting that Pessoa was made known to me through *Die Zeit*, a German language weekly although it has been Spanish and Portuguese scholars who have provided the access to his writings. Fate acts in mysterious ways; I am grateful to have obtained his writings, whatever the means.

Livro do Desassossego, Book of Discontent, is the great personal statement of the century. It compares with Rousseau's *Reveries* or Thoreau's *Journals* . Pessoa has gotten at the relationship of his soul to his material existence with uncompromising honesty and profound insight. He is one of those rare breeds who is equally philosopher and poet. He has been widely recognized in the latter role but few seem to take him seriously as a thinker. As far as I am concerned, the Portuguese literati can have his poetry, what the world at large needs is his prose.

Like most original thinkers of modern times, Pessoa died at a relatively young age. It is sobering for me to realize that he died at an age before which I had even started thinking in a serious manner. I must be realistic in my expectations for myself–not with respect to public recognition but as far as what I can expect myself to accomplish through writing.

* * *

I understand now that the essential ingredient missing in my personality is freedom from my society and the element of myself molded by it. Until one exorcises the harmful influences out of his spirit, he cannot be any good to himself or anyone else. For this exorcism, there is no substitute for a profound distrust of everything, including all the habits of the mind. When Antisthenes was asked what learning was most necessary, he replied "*to periairein, to apomanthanein*," which may be freely translated as the shedding of harmful mental baggage.

Although I have dealt with the cruder problems which plagued me in my youth–excessive ambition, excessive greed, excessive sexuality–I am yet bedeviled with other, more subtle disturbances which are undoubtedly part of the same baggage. There is a perpetual restlessness dwelling within me that is not my natural self and must be a consequence of perverted social programming.

I refuse to accept the cynicism that seems to be the lot of writers I know whose consciousness does not go beyond the materialist vision of the world. Merely because everything seems trivial to me or dishonest or both, or that literature, the final resting place of my aspirations, seems to me more and more a hypocritical game by which authors play the same role that priests and clowns played in earlier times; merely because I discover in myself the most repulsive habits of thought that are no better than those I despise except that they are covered over by a radical individualism; all this does not mean that a human being like myself cannot find a suitable place for his mind in the world. It only means that I have not yet learned where this place is to be found.

* * *

One thing that is absolutely impossible for me is to live like a mindless animal. The pleasures of the senses do not satisfy me for more time than it takes to register them in my brain. Nor does the adulation of another person, ten persons, a thousand persons, millions of persons; adulation has no more affect on me than walking out into a sunny day. The rays may feel good for a few seconds but it is the most transient of experiences. I have learned that the admiration of a crowd is a state that serves the admirers exclusively and is little related to the object of admiration. A public has no more basis for responding to my writings than did my mother when I wrote my first sentences in an elementary school composition class.

The naiveté of philosophers, positivists, psychoanalysts, naturalists and other systematizers lies in the fact that they are not sufficiently suspicious of themselves and their motives for teaching their own particular brand of wisdom. Most teachers are sophists, they reveal their knowledge for their own personal benefit; if not directly for lucre, then indirectly via prestige, adulation, fame and what have you. How can I take seriously the assertions of a person who benefits materially from his teachings or writings? One would think in a society sophisticated in concepts of business practice, the concept of "conflict of interest" would be understood with respect to public writings. At least when I go the circus or the theater, I understand I am being entertained for an admission fee. It seems to me that it was only the now extinct Puritans who understood the difficulties of getting at the truth of people. If I can't help smiling at their notion of a ubiquitous Satan, I can appreciate their awareness of the pervasiveness of human self-deception. It would be all to easy to ascribe my difficulties to the Devil if my intellectual conscience did not stand in the way.

One thing I do know is that I cannot believe anyone who tells me about the world outside instead of the one within himself.

Since the only lasting pleasure I have ever had in my life has been the development of my consciousness, it must be here that the key to my contentment is to be found.

* * *

The University of California provides me with an essential requirement for my development; a comprehensive library and access to books of all languages to serve my needs. A library is the centerpiece of any university and perhaps the only real resource that is necessary for it. I see crowds of students milling about during the day, traveling from room to room like players in a giant-sized monopoly game, thinking that the pursuit of an education terminates in the right classroom. How misguided they are and how absurd a system is that thinks education can be imparted through lectures and in classrooms. If it were left to me, most classroom activities would be abolished, leaving the professional schools to operate through the greatly superior apprentice system and liberal education to be acquired through discipleship The antique Greeks knew that the way one learned about the world–which is the object of liberal education–was through sharing the life of a wise man who could communicate his wisdom. Such were the schools of Athens. A library is a means for gaining access to wisdom that is remote in time and space; the whole secret of modern education is to know what books to read at what moments in one's life. I have known no wise men so I have had to spend inordinate amounts of time seeking them out in libraries.

The classrooms of the University could be profitably turned over to street entertainers who would then provide diversions to students who are engage in the arduous search for higher education.

* * *

I am a roamer of streets. However, I do not roam widely; I am not a *flaneur* of the Parisian or New York variety who is always exploring new vistas. My roaming is confined to five blocks of Telegraph Avenue in Berkeley, from Dwight to Sproul Plaza. I walk and rewalk these poor pavements without boredom or fatigue. There are more than enough bookstores, coffee houses, food stalls, outdoor performers, bizarre passers-by, poets, homeless, blacks, foreigners, students, teachers, panhandlers, schizophrenics, misfits and exhibitionists to satisfy my every whim for observation or pleasure. The world is at my feet on Telegraph Avenue; it is displeasing to me when I am forced to wander unfamiliar streets that are less satisfying to me than the ones I know. Even worse, is my occasional participation in "high" culture when I am forced to sit for several hours watching or listening to some sort of boring spectacle. The enigma of my life and of all existence is on display on Telegraph; if it cannot be resolved there, it cannot be resolved anywhere.

When my work for hire activities are completed or when I have had to engage in social intercourse for prolonged periods, Telegraph is my retreat. Once there, I breathe a sigh of relief, I am now in my proper relationship to the world, a free observer, a hunter and dipper into things of the mind, a man unencumbered by oppression. I come and go as I please and answer to no man for my time or behavior. It is on Telegraph Avenue that I work out the drama of my own life and my connection to what is around me.

If Telegraph Avenue is my world, my writing cubicle with its notebooks and typewriter is my art. Here the current is reversed, instead of taking in the world, I endeavor to create it. Fundamentally, I am a lazy person, inclined toward a talmudical type of scholarship that I suppose I have inherited from ancestors whose minds were formed in yeshivas of long gone communities in eastern Europe. Be that as it may, I am quite content in looking, reading, drinking, eating–basically taking in from my environment rather than acting upon it. This kind of relationship with the world tends to deteriorate in time and I find myself feeling like a voyeur instead of participant. A sense of ennui and dissipation occurs in me when I have been the *flaneur* too long. It is then that I return to my writing cubicle.

Sometimes it seems that writing for me represents an adjustment of my consciousness in which composition of prose relieves the tension of mind excessively distended. The essential I regains its dominance over the receptive and reflective activity which form so large a part of my waking hours. Similarly, I regard reading as a kind of receptive input into the mind, perhaps not in quite the pejorative sense of Schopenhauer who said reading was thinking with another's brain, but certainly as a kind of experience of the mind of another. Naturally one seeks out literary experiences which are congenial but the principle remains, reading is a borrowing from another's mental efforts. A constant input of this sort without reversing the direction of flow leads to pressure atrophy of the mind, a condition all too common among professional scholars. Writing for me thus is a *reparative* activity, analogous to animals tonguing their wounds clean or seeking solitude when they are ill.

Whether or not anyone reads my writings is an entirely different matter. "If it happens, it will be good, if doesn't happen, it will also be good." Such was the enlightened attitude of Pessoa toward a readership for his own work.

* * *

The composition of a piece of writing is an important event for me. My ability to express myself in my own voice was a development in my life at least equal to my learning to walk and talk. When my thoughts emerge on the printed page, it is much like the first time I was able to traverse a room on my own two feet although I cannot remember exactly how I felt on that occasion. I am sure, however, there was a similar thrill of accomplishment. When I write, I not only walk, I swim, fly, run, engage in all manner of movements on a mental level. I advance beyond the animal state into the singularity of the human condition whereby one's consciousness is objectified. This is the real purpose of my writing; the creation of a personal experience exercising my spirit, and through so doing, creating its own being. Then I become the *real I*, I become the *I* am that *I* am, *I* overcome the world. Nature, Culture, Civilization, Eternity–all are facets of one existence that serve to enhance my being.

The more structured my writing is according to literary convention, the less it serves the purpose proclaimed above. If I write poetry, the problem of language assumes the preeminent position in my mind, the *I* retreats to a backroom position. When writing essays, I become a critic, a savant, or an entertainer; positions which are far removed from my own true self. I once wrote a novel which took me six months and almost destroyed my sense of writing as being centered on myself rather than unknown readers. I will say nothing about the aberrations of my former career as a scientist in which my writings were akin to the work of bookkeepers maintaining the records of a giant corporation.

The freer I feel in the act of writing, the more likely it is that the final product will reflect my reality. I cannot write more than a few pages at a time; after that, what emerges is the product of mental discipline rather than the ebullitions of my spirit. One must not think it is easy elaborating thoughts into written language; it is difficult but it is enlivening and it liberates one from having to be a slave to the conventions of a materialist society. The main thing is to regard writing to be in the service of the soul–as long as that idea is clear, everything else will follow.

* * *

My life is like a river flowing somewhere even though I often have difficulty in determining the direction of flow. Yet there is no doubt in my mind that it is after something. As I look back on its turns and twists, its sudden changes of direction, its accelerations and periods of stagnation, I am struck by the relentless flow. It is going somewhere.

I can honestly say that all my life, I have been seeking to develop the interior consciousness which I call the soul. All the activities, all the reading, studying, writing, all the pursuit of evanescent insights have been exercises in the development of my consciousness. I do not say there is anything admirable in such a life, it is merely the life I have been compelled to live. As Thoreau said, "I respect my aspirations if not always my activities." Development of consciousness has always been my aspiration, and, always, if I have been too long diverted from this goal, I have found ways to return to it.

The writers I have admired have had a single-minded dedication to express their consciousness. They have been inveterate city dwellers or lovers of nature, possessors of a tranquil disposition or subject to restlessness and *Angst*, prolific writers or writers of a few aphorisms, atheists, theists, bachelors, parents, rarely healthy, commonly sickly, long-lived, short-lived, in short, they have had mental and physical features of every type. But what they all have in common is an orientation toward the interior self as contrasted to an orientation to society. They had reverence for their own souls.

I am not a man of physical action. Whenever I am confronted with a task requiring my engagement in the material world, I must grit my teeth and prepare to do battle with my own nature. It is as if I feel that involvement with the concrete is offensive in some way–not that I think it is below me in an aristocratic sense, it is rather that I feel that object-oriented activity is alien to my own being. The men of action in this world seem like great ugly dinosaurs blundering about in a jungle, they may accomplish their ends but I am put off by their grossness.

If one single thought becomes clearer to me as a result of an hour's labor at my typewriter, the writing was worthwhile. If there were a more effective way that I could enhance myself other than writing, I would certainly leap at the chance. But I have never discovered any alternatives to involvement with the written word.

$$* * *$$

All my life I have fought to stay free of tribalism. Tribalism is the enemy, the foe that drains my energies and crushes my spirit. In the beginning of my life, my enemy was the tribalism of my old family, later it was of my new family. My schools, my professions, my religion, my family connections–all have attempted in subtle or not-so subtle ways to capture my spirit, preventing my own self from flourishing.

Tribalism means that an external order of things is the dominant value in thought and action. Tribalism means that one's values are focused outside rather than within. We superior beings of the western world look with amused condescension at primitives caught up in primitive tribal mores but I do not see that the educated westerner living out his life dominated by machines is any different from the primitive. It is not technology that determines the superiority of the human species, it is the ability to evolve a consciousness of profounder realities than those of the physical universe. Is there anyone who really believes that, as a human being, Henry Thoreau was not superior to Henry Ford?

Tribalism is the enemy of the self because it fundamentally stands for the self subordinated to external circumstance. Whether it be a tyrannical parent, a demanding career or an adulatory public; the one who gives himself over to the exterior organization of his life is incapable of developing his interior self. The self does not develop through intellectual exercises, it develops through the demands of solitary existence, the only existence the self knows. It is the process of giving oneself over to something external which is destructive of it.

Sitting here at my writing table, searching my soul for the treasure within it, straining to express what has previously been only a dim and clouded feeling, knowing that no one else is looking over my shoulder—it is then that I am ministering to my self, bringing it slowly toward new vistas, acting in my own genuine best interests and defeating all the tribalisms which seek to prevent me from moving beyond the animal state into the condition of being *Homo sapiens*.

* * *

No life can be led without creating a hierarchical structure of values. The cultivation of the interior self is at the pinnacle of this hierarchy, but a human being who is flesh as well as spirit must care for all aspects of his existence. Fanaticism is the denial of the hierarchical structure of existence. It is necessary for me to look to the needs of my body and my social nature; I must have proper nutrition, shelter, exercise and human intercourse. I could not bear to beg for daily needs nor could I permit myself to be shut up and cared for like an animal in a zoo. The needs of my interior self can coexist with my biological and psychological needs; what it cannot endure is an inferior status to them. Thoreau wrote that "there is no more fatal blunderer than he who consumes the greater part of his life in gaining a living" but it is not the time spent which is the issue but rather a misconceived system of values that puts what should be above below and raises the bottom to the top.

* * *

When I discovered the prose writings of Fernando Pessoa, I was like a person mesmerized. I read them side by side in Spanish and Portuguese since at first I could not fully understand Pessoa's Portuguese without the excellent Spanish translation of Angel Crespo. It was as though I could never tire of Pessoa's thoughts, never get enough exposure to his mind. Most writers bore me quickly so that I am rarely able to finish a novel or maintain interest very long in casual non-fiction prose. But Pessoa never fails to exert a spell over me and I have probably spent dozens of hours on *Livro do Desassossego*–and will probably spend dozens more.

What is it about Pessoa's writings that mesmerizes me? It is not a case of hero worship since I do not rate his personality very highly nor do I admire his style of living. Because of his exclusively literary orientation, Pessoa missed out on essential experiences that go into a human life. He wrote too much about things he knew little about, he would have done well to have more focus in his work. His poetical works seem to me to be over-sentimentalized and too much concerned with language rather than with content. There is certainly little to be said for his juvenile occultism or his Portuguese chauvinism. As a model of a writer or of as a human being, I do not rank him highly.

Yet I forgive Pessoa all his shortcomings because he has achieved something in his writings that is rarely found in western literature. *Pessoa has reverence for his soul* and has centered his writing upon it, discarding the cultural dead weight that burden the work of so many other writers. One need only to compare his writings with that of Gottfried Benn or Sartre for example, to see what it really means to take one's soul seriously. Pessoa is not catering to the literary establishment when he writes, he is not encumbered by litterateurism, he genuinely cares about the state of his interior self. He brings a unique passion to letters–that of an individual determined to pay attention to his own self through his writings. One can only find his equivalent in Thoreau, Nietzsche and the elderly Rousseau, perhaps Marcus Aurelius and Amiel should also be included. I cannot think of any other individuals who have raised *creative* writing to such heights.

* * *

The true nature of my interior self is a being in constant change, change of mood, change of emotion, change of thought. It is like an ameboid organism perpetually changing configuration with long fingers of protoplasm extending and withdrawing according to circumstance. That is why it is difficult for me to write extended essays about serious matters–I am never quite the same person at each sitting during which I write. My truest writings are those which emerge entirely in one effort because they wholly reflect the self in existence at the time they were composed. I shudder to think of ever again writing a book with an organized theme because of the deformation my soul endures through such a process.

Change is an essential aspect of all life, including human life. If I do not feel each day of my life that I am a different person in some way, I sense stagnation and am disappointed in myself. The problem with aging is that it becomes more difficult with each passing year to discover the experiences conducive to change. When I discover a literary work that is truly significant to me–a writing of any sort, even a sentence will do–then I am a man alive and will peruse over and over again the words which have given me a new sense of being. I struggled to learn to read Portuguese in order to have access to Pessoa–I would learn Arabic or Japanese if I thought a similar experience would be forthcoming. Pessoa said that the

Portuguese were the most civilized people in the world because they are the people most open to change. I doubt his premise but believe that the idea is correct; I feel myself to be "civilized" to the degree I can incorporate change into my inner being.

* * *

"ETERNAL RECURRENCE"

I am the last human being. All culture, all civilization, all the efforts of all the races of humanity have terminated in me. It is my duty to justify all that has gone before me because there may be nothing after me. Posterity is a word without significance, analogous to words like God, heaven, hell and all the myriad of concepts humans have used to lift the burden of responsibility for their life from their own shoulders. Everything must be justified by my own existence because after me there is the empty void of non-being. My own consciousness is the *ultimate reality*, the end toward which all the efforts of my life has been directed. My art has been created in order to create my own soul, it has no other purpose. Out of the non-being of tribal life, I have emerged as this final reality, an end unto myself.

* * *

It is incomprehensible to me how people believe an artwork can be more important than the artist who created it. Who imagines that man can be more important than his Creator? Every creative personality is in some way aware that he is enhanced by his creative activities even though he may be exhausted by them. However, the public and the critics share a compulsion for idol worship in which the importance of the work created is exaggerated while the artist as human being is ignored.

As a human being, I am quite sure that I am more important than any of my writings. Anyone who reads my work and does not experience my personality has wasted his time. What is real is my spirit alive and functioning at this moment in time; what I write is a projection of my being and why I write is the desire to augment that being. There is no meaning to my writing except as a sign of my existence at a particular crossroads in time and in space. My writing is like a flag fluttering over a city, signifying a presence to all who understand its significance.

Once one has gotten the tribal instinct under control and liberated his individuality, he no longer needs to devote himself to his society. There is nothing more tragic than for a potentially great-souled person to expend all his energies in tribal affairs at the expense of his own inner being. What is important is that he become conscious of his own nature as an independent entity. He may not, as Heraclitus maintained, ever be able to explore the utmost limits of the self but he will at least have the satisfaction of knowing he has undertaken the journey.

* * *

Once again . . . I am unknown, my writings do not entertain, I instruct no one in any aspect of living. My work is not publishable since there is no reason to suspect a market exists for them. None of this disturbs me since my writing is a personal activity and needs no curious onlookers. Just as I do not need bystanders when I run for exercise, so I need no readers looking over my shoulder at my writings.

* * *

My mind seems to be in perpetual motion, the less that objectively happens to me, the more active it becomes. In fact, I have become aware that I cannot endure the condition of prolonged *engagement* in which my mind is reduced to the level of problem-solving. Whenever this occurs for more than a little while, I disengage.

I am a person who rarely looks back. Others whom I meet are always looking back, forever ruminating on the events of the past and reliving their past experiences. But I live in the future, always

I am anticipating some forthcoming event or change in my condition. The present is generally of little interest to me since what is happening now no longer requires my mental energies. There are occasional exceptions but they are infrequent. By and large, in order for something to hold my interest, there has to be an element of becoming relieving the tedium of the already being.

* * *

Recently, I read some passages from the writings of Gottfried Benn. At one time, I would have been captivated by his wit, his learning, his European refinement. But I have passed beyond interest in litterateurism. If a writer cannot give me his interior self, I am not interested. It did not surprise me to learn that Benn, like Heidegger, threw himself into the first phases of the Nazi regime in Germany. It is harder for German writers to liberate themselves from their culture than for any other language group. The weight of "Germanism" seems to be overwhelming, one has only to compare Nietzsche, Mann, Adorno, Benn, etc. With Kierkegaard, Unamuno, Thoreau or Pessoa to feel the difference.

* * *

The other day I saw a wonderful production of *Peer Gynt*. Yet three-quarters of the audience could not sit through an already abbreviated version. There seemed to be no interest in most of the onlookers in the problem of existence that Peer Gynt poignantly demonstrates. Today's audiences do not seem to be able to relish anything except the fast moving pap that is the usual offering of the performing arts. It is hard to imagine that overflowing ancient Greek audiences sat through several works of Sophocles in a single day.

I do not know of any play of Ibsen's as meaningful as *Peer Gynt*. It would be interesting to learn more about what Ibsen himself thought of his character. Surely he did not believe the problem of existence could be solved by throwing oneself into the lap of an acquiescent girl. But Ibsen abandoned the problem of existence for the problems of women, politics, society, etc. A pity.

* * *

Most writers write too much. It becomes the sole form of expression that they are capable of taking seriously. I hope not to fall into that trap. My writing has the purpose of developing myself; I am not in the service of my writing. It is hard for me to comprehend how society has come to value the art object over the artist. It is idol worship in which artists should not collude just because of the lucre or ego gratification. The gigantic novels, poems, treatises produced by the literati of past ages merely feed into the public's thirst for literary monuments that can serve to replace physical monuments. *War and Peace* is to me a kind of Great Pyramid of Cheops; except that it was only Tolstoy who exhausted himself in its creation instead of armies of slaves. (One should not forget that Tolstoy, always the sincerest of writers, came to repudiate all of his immense novels.)

* * *

The lack of recognition as a writer has been the most powerful motivator toward my development in this capacity. Since the outside world does not regard me as a person with a literary profession, the continued application of myself in this direction has required me to search out the meaning of my impetus to write. The blessing of literary isolation is that it shields one from the false warmth of societal acceptance. At the present time, it is hard for me to imagine myself as a person with a literary reputation. It would be a threat to my independence, to the sense of reality I have about my interior self. There is a certain intimacy I have found in my isolation as a writer that I would be reluctant to part with. However, there seems to be no danger of such a development at this time.

The writer who has or expects a reading public–no matter how small–is in a different position than one who does not. No matter how cynical he may appear to be about his readership, he cannot avoid being influenced by the fact of its existence. He wants to give satisfaction. He cannot write for himself alone because he knows his work will affect others who have expectations from him. His public, his publisher, his own circumstances and those who are connected with him will be affected by the reception of his writing. Just as it is an illusion to think that a *paterfamilias* with a dependent wife and children can be as free as a person without family obligations, so it is an illusion to think that a writer who has "arrived" is free to work out his own existence in his writing.

The question of literary "success" is the most important issue that an individual who is writing for his own soul must face. The ancients believed that the problem of fame was "the last infirmity of the noble mind." It is not merely a matter of an economic situation or ego gratification but a matter of one's orientation to life. Metaphysical awareness is required to deal with the problem of fame because it is closely linked to the underlying problem of existence. The person who finds his place in life through the attitudes of others is one who has not worked through the reality of his own individuality. Hypocrisy is rampant in this regard; everywhere there are those who sneer at public adulation but who themselves cannot dispense with it. The question posed by Rousseau's Savoyard Vicar about philosophers is a universal one for writers; would they write if they were required to publish anonymously, forever relinquishing the possibility of personal rewards.

The problem of fame I perceive as only the last of a series of manifestations of the tribal instinct in me, grounded in the desire to merge into an extended group instead of establishing my independence as an individual. Literary fame is very close to military fame (as the old soldier Cervantes pointed out); it is also little different from fame as a politician, professional craftsman or circus performer. Every famous person sees himself as a member of an elite club standing above the common herd. For those with no special skill, there is the elitism of birthright or culture or family traditions. It is all tribalism, the yearning to find reality in group identification instead of one's own self. It is a rejection of the destiny of the human being to become spiritually independent. From this perspective, it is difficult to believe that the human race is currently evolving in a desirable manner.

Sitting at my desk in front of my typewriter, experiencing thoughts which flow from my mind onto the sheet of paper in front of me, it is crystal clear to me where my reality is to be found. The best of me is in full flower at this moment, what happens later amidst the superficial social scene will be a falling-off. Little by little, I have tried to nurture this reality and shed my tribal instincts. I am convinced that fame is properly a posthumous phenomenon and that notoriety for a writer before he dies is like subjecting him to an autopsy before the life is out of the body. No amount of compensation is worth this mortification.

What I need is not fame but the mental energy to make something of myself and to correct the botched job of my upbringing.

* * *

I am surrounded by writers who are committed to the poetical form of literary expression. Everywhere in the San Francisco Bay area are poetry readings, poetry publications, poetry assemblies. One of the main reasons for my literary isolation is my lack of empathy with this form of writing. My interest in writing is entirely a product of the desire to express my ideas about things; it seems to me that in poetry, ideas take second place. Poets are writers who are primarily interested in language just as painters are interested in appearances and musicians in sound. I know that there are often ideas of great import expressed poetically. Yet somehow I have the feeling that the esthetics of language is more important to the poet than the ideas or emotions that they express. I find it quite significant that I can readily read prose in several languages other than my native one but am unable to comprehend poetry in any of them. One does not need a perfect acquaintanceship with a language in order to grasp the ideas in prose writing but a lack of intimate familiarity with the structure and style of an idiom defeats any attempt to appreciate its poetry. Poetry is bound up with sound and style, prose merely utilizes these things to convey thoughts. Poetry, I believe, is essentially untranslatable from one language to another; prose can be readily translated and often gains much through a good translation.

Since it is ideas not esthetics that draw me to literature, I find myself impatient with poetry and maintain the same superficial relationship to it that I have with painting or music. The agenda I have for literary activity does not include elevating the language. It is the expression of self that I look for and since my concept of humans is that they are thinking beings, what I want to know about them is what they think. This means apprehending their ideas. Literature provides me with the opportunity of experiencing the ideas of people who interest me.

Fernando Pessoa, who was both an accomplished poet and a great writer of prose, expressed the view that since poetry represented an early phase of linguistic appreciation, it would become obsolete when humans reached higher levels of development. Not being a poet, it would be presumptuous of me to endorse his opinion. I merely note that poetry falls into a different category of literary expression than prose, one in which ideas take a subordinate position.

* * *

My life has been blighted by a series of circumstances that has taken me many years of intense retrospection to unravel. I have identified three main factors that were preeminently involved in obliterating my spirit. It may be that I exaggerate somewhat in trying to define these factors but it is necessary that I be unsparing in facing reality. It is better to err on the side of exaggeration than to overlook noxious influences unnoticed because of their long-standing presence.

The first factor that blighted my life was the attitude of my entire family. I arose out of a generation that ruthlessly extirpated all spiritual values for the sake of adaptation to a foreign culture. Having freed themselves from a superannuated and spiritually defunct Judaism, my parents were in no mood to encourage me toward any other type of spiritual values, whether it is the long feared Christianity of the surrounding society or the free-wheeling spirituality of the creative arts. What I was expected to do was to equip myself to function successfully in a materialist culture. Science was the God of my family and it was to training in a scientific profession that they looked to provide entree into the good like in America. Never did I imagine in my formative years that the problems of life could be solved in any way except through some kind of technological training. Never did I seriously consider that there might be something within me that would not be satisfied by the big three of bourgeois living—career, family and a comfortable estate. I undertook, without any reservations, to devote my entire life to one of the scientific professions available to an ambitious young man. This resulted in approximately twenty-five years of living in which I continually anticipated that I would find happiness—or at least a reasonable degree of contentment. I achieved success but the expected happiness or contentment never followed. In fact, the more success I achieved, the more unhappy and discontent I became. The presence of wife, children, friends, home, affluence availed me nothing. My life was blighted and continues to be blighted by that twenty-five years in the arid wilderness of bourgeois living.

The second adverse factor in my life has been my country, or more specifically, the intellectual and moral values that exist within it. Feeling from the beginning that bourgeois living lacked some vital factor, I periodically looked about for some other path I might take. Only occasionally in literature, I uncovered the thinking of people who had something inspiring to say to me and who realized that human life was more than a career and family nest. However I found nothing in my own milieu to serve as any kind of model to me. On the one hand, there was the relentless careerism for which my family had prepared me–if not scientific careerism, than some other kind whether it be in business, the professions or academia. Whatever one did, financial remuneration was the bottom line and if it were not forthcoming, the endeavor was not worth the effort. This was the result of living in the most materialist country of a world where materialism is triumphant everywhere. On the other hand, the traditional non-materialist influence, the Christian religion, never seemed more to me than fairy tales for children–or worse, if one believes Nietzsche. I follow Thoreau in that my deity is reality; whatever cannot persuade me of the reality of its being is of no value to me. To the extent that my society has failed to expose me to believable spiritual values, it has contributed to the blighting of my life.

Finally, there is a third factor, quite likely the most important of them all, that has negatively impacted on my life. This is my own weakness, my lack of sufficient determination to find my own path from the onset. I am struck by amazement and envy at hearing about lives of those who in their twenties, even teenage years, had the courage and resourcefulness to find their own way in life and assert their souls regardless of lack of encouragement by their society. I was never able to behave in such a way. Even at this time in my life, when I am propped up by financial and institutional supports of every kind, I find it difficult to act according to my convictions. I fear that my character has been damaged by the combination of an inherent cowardice and a lack of external guidance oriented to my real needs. There can never be a fully integrated I which will stand forth reflecting its own purity, regardless of what surrounds it. But at least I can record the situation of my life as I see it–perhaps others may benefit from my sad plight.

* * *

The other day, a friend asked me how my books were distributed. When I replied that I distributed them myself to whomever I thought was interested in them, he became uncomfortable as if he had opened a door that should have remained closed. It was obvious that he thought my lack of a professional distributor was evidence of my lack of literary success, akin to hearing a shopkeeper confess that no one enters his shop. He tried to conceal his reaction but it was clear that my response had embarrassed him. He could not imagine that the absence of sales of my books would not be a painful subject for me.

I find that very few people have any sense of the rewards of writing unconnected to a public. People understand how one can derive satisfaction from ascending to the top of a mountain peak or navigating a perilous river but they seem to be unable to carry over the same concept to the process of writing. I suppose that this is so because so many writers associate the rewards of their work with obtaining a public readership (and therefore monetary remuneration) that there is now a reflex reaction that one writes for readers. Malcolm Cowley once wrote that an author is a writer with readers–all writers want to be "authors." I cannot deny that this feeling has existed in me and at times returns unexpectedly although as I gain experience, becoming more sure of myself as a writer, the satisfactions of writing for its intrinsic rewards becomes more firmly established.

Just why do writers want readers? For the professional writer, the answer is evident–the need to make a living from sales of one's writings. This motivation requires little comment, it is the same one which impels any professional person to seek out clients; one cannot support oneself in a profession without gaining adequate monetary recompense. A great many writers dream of supporting themselves through their writings; thus the acquisition of readers becomes the key element underlying their feeling of success as a writer. They are not content to be writers, they wish to be professional writers, i.e., to derive their livelihoods from their writings.

Aside from the matter of compensation, there are many writers who are primarily attracted by the prestige connected with being a writer who has a following. There is something about the feeling that one's books sell which provides a powerful boost to self-esteem. Furthermore, writers are all too ready to believe that their writings have a beneficial effect upon their readers. Such writers may be principally rewarded by the acclaim and notoriety with lesser attention paid to financial aspects of writing. Of course, fame and notoriety are relative terms. The few thousand readers that would delight some writers would be abject failure for others. I have a degree of fame and notoriety among a dozen or so readers drawn from my family and friends. However, this degree of celebrity would hardly suffice for most writers who desire a wider public.

Now there are some writers who do not exactly crave notoriety but still require a certain degree of "recognition" in order to feel validated in their writing. They wish the approval of those who are in a position to know about quality writing in their area. They require the approval of experts or connoisseurs–such as the approval given to fine wines or high fashion clothing. Naturally, a large reading public enhances this kind of recognition but is not as necessary as it is to those who yearn for celebrity status.

For myself, I find that writing with absolutely no desire for readers of any kind is what is best for me. Many of the Greek philosophers who lived in societies highly oriented toward celebrity status came to share this feeling. *Lathé bios*–live unknown–was Epicurus' prescription for a fulfilling life. Even early, Antisthenes maintained that pain and obscurity were the two conditions required for the development of the inner self. I am not sure about pain but obscurity is an absolute necessity.

I write to bring into objective being that which is within me, not to divert or instruct others. There is a birthing involved in writing, I deliver my interior self into the light, my soul makes itself known to any who will see, what can emerge in no other way emerges when I sit down to write. Some instinct, beyond that of survival or procreation, drives me to express my experience of the world. What purpose is served by reviewers, critics or a reading public in this instinctual act? None, I no more need a public to write than I need one to breathe, eat or copulate. Breathing and eating keep my body alive, copulation keeps the race alive but writing nourishes my soul outranking my other instincts because it elevates me above the beasts. All genuinely expressive activity nourishes the soul. Every human being has within him a soul requiring such nourishment; however, it is only the more determined ones who have the will to engage in this task.

* * *

The desire for riches is more individualized, and therefore on a higher level, than is the desire for fame. A person who is striving to enrich himself is one who is has a concept of himself as an independent individual. It may represent various aspects of the psyche; i.e., desire for accomplishment, for independence, for experiences, even for enjoying gamesmanship in the world of business. By and large, the desire for riches has been overly maligned among individuals; in my opinion, it is a manifestation of a highly developed individuality albeit perhaps in a direction needing modification.

On the other hand, the desire for fame or recognition is a manifestation of a personality that has failed to mature. The person who cannot be happy unless he is well thought of by his contemporaries resembles a schoolboy who requires high grades in order to feel secure. Much of the population of the world of science, arts and letters fall into this category. Many a writer is miserable unless he has received some measure of recognition by those whom he regards as his peers. This phenomenon merely indicates that tribalism exists in the most sophisticated circles. Nor can I exclude such a state in myself–after so much reflection on the subject, I find myself still watching my mailbox for evidence that I am an important person!

* * *

It appears to me that there has been a diminution in the spiritual force of humans during the past century. Where are the Beethovens, Kierkegaards, Nietzsches, Van Goghs or Gauguins of former times? While the human race has greatly proliferated and its material strength has been immeasurably increased by technology, the force of the individual human spirit has weakened. No doubt this is due to the ever-increasing reliance on machines but I believe it is also due to the increasing world population. If there is a finite quantity of spiritual energy accessible to our species, the more individuals there are on the planet, the less of it any one of them is likely to acquire. Physical energy is not an inexhaustible resource, I cannot see why spiritual energy should be any different. If we humans are so heedless as to multiply ourselves limitlessly (one need only to look at the soaring population figures of our planet for the past few centuries), then we must expect our current spiritual impoverishment. There are no machines to strengthen the spirit. It is ironical that spiritually defunct people, searching for causes to espouse, should have settled on "the right to life." What about the right to interior development?

* * *

When all is said and done, the critical question to be asked of a human is whether his life reflects respect for his own soul–not the souls of others, not the concept of a soul, not the soul as it has been imagined by religious dogmas–but his own soul evolved through his own experiences, which is the only one that can have real meaning for a person. I live an isolated life because I have little interest in people who do not think this way. Animal spirits cannot substitute for respect for one's soul.

My friend, who is a great idealist in everyday matters, is attuned to political or economic issues that might lead to a better life for people at large. His orientation is entirely practical, entirely on the surface of things. To me, he has missed the essential quality of the human condition which is consciousness of self, independent of utilitarian considerations. He glides along on the covering of the earth, unaware that the significant events occur underneath it. For this reason, his conversation quickly becomes boring to me and I am able to spend only limited time periods with him.

I have a great interest in the Puritan settlers who once lived in this country. They knew something about the soul; I do not believe American society has ever regained the spiritual depth that they conferred upon it. It is not necessary to be excessively preoccupied with their Christian fables although even those are more palatable to me than the current materialistic madness. I certainly don't approve of witch hunts (they later regretted them). But they knew there was something more inside a person than his internal organs, they were not subject to the state of mind that imagines we are made up exclusively of tangible and visible things. If America could have held on to the Puritan spirituality while dispensing with its childish Christian dogmas—which is what the Concord transcendentalists tried to do—this country might now be a better place. Instead, Ben Franklin became a national idol, followed by the likes of Thomas Edison, Henry Ford and Ronald Reagan. Now look what has become of us—talking heads lost in a materialist frenzy, the laughing-stock of all thoughtful men and the image of everything that is wrong with the modern world.

* * *

I am not interested in "advancing the language" as I was once advised to do by a well-meaning editor. "The language" serves the purpose of expressing my ideas, it has no value to me aside from this function. I have no ambitions to be as is said in Laertiana of Plato, "A sweet-voiced speaker, pouring out prose equal in delicacy to the cicada perched upon the trees of Hecademus." All my efforts in utilizing language are directed toward its most efficient usage in the expression of ideas. Embellishments and exaggerations that do not promote this purpose seem to me to reveal the decadence of the times. I would rather had Emerson say that what was needed for the person who aspires to improve his life was plain writing and high thinking.

Poetry to my mind is an inappropriate vehicle for a thinker since the purpose of poetry is so enmeshed with embellishing language. It may be true that historically poetry has expressed significant thoughts but the poet always labors under the handicap of attending to the sound and rhythm of his writing. Without this factor, he would create prose instead of poetry. It is difficult enough to bring one's thoughts into being through the written word, but the difficulty is even greater with poetry. The esthetics of poetical expression are not conducive to genuine expression of the mind.

I find it difficult to take poetry seriously except as a means for charming listeners or readers, something that I think is already sufficiently done in our society through other means. Basically, it seems to me to be better suited for the immature mind needing the soothing or stimulating effect of rhythms in order to sustain interest–much as an infant needs to be soothed or stimulated by its mother. Lucretius, the last of the philosopher-poets, refers to his poetry as honey needed to make his thoughts more palatable. Really profound poets like Baudelaire, Poe or Pessoa resorted to prose when they had something of definite consequence to themselves to write down.

* * *

I continue to search for the proper relationship to my society with respect to the real *me*, the me that thinks and writes. Being invisible as a literary person, my only connection with the literary world is as a consumer, that is to say as a reader of works that the arbiters of culture have deemed fit to make generally available. This is a quite arbitrary means of relating myself to society; writers and their writings becoming known to me through chance judgments determined by unpredictable events manipulated by total strangers. Writings that I find meaningful come to me the same way as accidents of nature; unpredictably and without conforming to any rational scheme. The experiences of my mind are subject to the literary fates just as my body is to natural fate, neither one or the other is subject to my control. Thus the world of literature which I delve into is quite like the natural world in which I live, both have to do with circumstances not of my choosing. There have surely been many profound minds to which I have had no access, in spite of my knowledge of many languages and my voracious reading habits. I have had to be satisfied with what fate has brought my way.

The situation is quite different with respect to myself as a writer. In this regard, I am an independent being who is full control of my relations to society. The opinions of the arbiters of culture is irrelevant to me since I do not write for them or those who put stock in their judgments. Nor do I depend on anonymous readers; that mass of humanity with no real relationship to me. Since I write only to develop myself, that determines my relationship to society. Should the arbiters of culture at some time change my invisible position to a visible one, it will not affect me as a writer– except perhaps expose me to some inconveniences. Thus my relationship as a literary person to society–as is the case of every independent person whose writings are self-expressive–is as a consumer but not as a producer of literature.

The greatest danger to the individual who writes is the concept of humanity. The most original and individualistic of writers often labor under the delusion that somehow their writings must seep through to humanity, or at least some segment of it. It is not enough for them to cultivate their interior selves; societal contempt for solitary individuals soaks into their minds, inculcating them with the feeling that in some way every writer should cater to humanity. Thus emerges the combination of hubris and self-denigration that is manifest in the desire for fame. It is impossible to imagine how much of perversion of self has occurred as a result of this tendency. Literature will never really amount to anything as long as writers are chained to the worship of anonymous masses, i.e., to the procuring of a reading public.

* * *

The hallmark of the inner self is abstract thought; when my writing has to do with abstractions, I know that I am expressing what is within me. The moment I begin to write about concrete things such as the details of my living situation, my surroundings, my relationships or the specifics of my bodily existence, I am wandering away from what is really me. The primary characteristic of the soul is intangibility so that it is only natural that intangible thought is its proper expression. Plotinus would not allow his portrait to be painted because he did not want to distract his followers from his ideas. One becomes concrete out of the need to be entertaining; i.e., to obtain a public. Since I have long given up interest in a public, I rarely have need to include concretisms in my writing.

Along the same line of thought, I am interested in the fact that there has always been a tendency to separate literary from spoken language. Spoken language is the repository of the concrete, the biological, the tangible elements of human existence while in literary language, abstraction is preeminent. This must be why it is easy for me to learn to read languages whereas I am incapable of more than halting conversation in any idiom except the one with which I grew up. It is fortunate that I at least learned to speak English as a child, otherwise I might be utterly without speech with all the difficulties that mutism entails. The motivation is not there for me to learn another set of spoken representations of concrete things.

Could it be that the abandonment of Latin–a language dead to the world of daily spoken intercourse–as the preferred medium of literary communication was a turning downward of European culture? Has there been anyone whose written thought has approached the profundities of Spinoza's Latin writings? It is said that Spinoza feared public opprobrium but why really did he refuse to allow his work to be translated into the Dutch vernacular?

Nevertheless, encumbered as we are by languages that serve our bodies as well as our souls, we must make the best of the situation. Pessoa distinguished his life in the Portuguese language from his life among the Portuguese people. It has always been so for self-directed writers. Without a dualistic orientation, regardless of the underlying, unpenetrable reality, the flourishing of *Homo sapiens* as a self-conscious being is untenable. Thus since we live in an era which is monistic to the core, we are witnessing the steady deterioration of spiritual consciousness. For this reason, persons of spirit feel archaic, out of place, their thoughts "out of season," and sooner or later, they yearn to depart from a society that they find hostile to the essence of their being.

Rereading Baudelaire's *Mon Coeur Mis A Nu*, I wonder if I am guilty of plagiarism?

* * *

The most difficult of all tasks for humans is to develop their souls. There are a million distractions lurking in every corner which impede this development. Everywhere enticements exist to lead the individual away from self and toward the external world. The developed soul has no currency in society. There is not one element of societal education that is genuinely oriented toward elevating consciousness. What is called by that name is invariably just another form of mass culture with orientation of self toward pleasure, success or adaptation to one's milieu.

Always I find myself in a struggle with a society that is continually trying to divert my attention. Being a person with many weaknesses, I am susceptible to outside pressures. How difficult it is sustain a steady focus on my inner being and not be diverted by social lures. It is so hard not to remain a child, obediently following the rules of games organized by unknown forces. It strikes me how little mental discipline is required to participate in a cause, work for a social end, or assist another toward presumed desirable goals. One is always looking for the authority of someone else's idea to gain self-confidence.

But no matter how tempting programmed activities may be, there is always a voice within me telling me I am reverting to childhood, succumbing to the seductions of society, turning my back on what I know is the only reality worth working for–the development of myself. And then I turn again to my mind, seeing and thinking with that great internal eye which is the I. And then I turn to divine literature, the only means of self-realization in a world that is more and more dehumanized with the passing of every year.

* * *

I have an invariably reliable criterion to determine if a creative activity pertains to the soul. It is similar to how Socrates defined the sophists of his day. It is whether or not MONEY is involved in the activity. If money changes hands as a result of a certain activity, I know the activity is a business and, therefore, by definition, is not a manifestation of the soul of the individual. If one engages in an activity for monetary reward, then the activity is necessarily an aspect of society and not of internal development.

* * *

The internal self is the final frontier of humanity. All lands have been explored, there is now only tourist circuses conducting people like locusts over all surfaces of the globe. Outer space is useless as a frontier, there is no new life or land to discover except barren rock and it will only make individuals more dependent than ever upon a soulless technology. More and more, science and scholarship tend to breed analytic robots whose human features shrivel into nothingness. Only the emergence of a soul offers something of enduring interest; without this "frontier," there remain merely the choices between alcohol, depression or suicide, all of which are rampant in the society. There is evolving, however, according to good Darwinian principles, a population for whom automatic living is *de rigueur*. The rest of us are being threatened by overpopulation of the world with aging children without souls, concerned only with the prolongation of an increasingly automatized existence.

Until the institutionalized western religions are firmly retired and consigned to museums of anthropology, and their founders seen for what they really were, episodes in the history of human development, it is unlikely that our society will create conditions which promote spiritual unfolding. Like dogs in a manger, our religions neither fructify nor permit others to be fructified. At the present moment, however, society seems to be moving in the other direction and "ministers" of every stripe dominate the public mind. The "metaphysics of the masses" is now the only metaphysics to be found.

* * *

What is consciousness as distinguished from stimulus-response existence? Merely developing awareness of reality–nothing more. Lower animals react to stimuli, *Homo sapiens* becomes conscious of them. In this simple formulation, lies the sense of direction of my existence. To become conscious of stimuli instead of reacting to them–that is a goal worthy of effort.

How does one become conscious of stimuli? By trusting reflection to lead one out of societal stimulus-response prisons into the life of the mind. By ignoring biologists who, true to their reductionist compulsions, tell us that consciousness is the illusion of complex neuronal activity underlying stimulus-response phenomena. Above all, by choosing the life of the mind to remaining in that most absurd and contemptible of all conditions, the physically mature, mentally infantile human being.

Art is the activity in which human consciousness is manifest;

of all art forms, literature is the one that is most worthy of manifesting it. Literature permits the individual to enter into the mind of other conscious beings and to participate in that most remarkable event, the *objectivization of consciousness*.

* * *

The writings of interest to me are those which project the inner self of the writer. I am aware that the reason this kind of writing is available to me is because the writer's fame has led to the preservation of his works. No Athens without Alexandria. If Baudelaire had not become famous through the criminal prosecution of his *Fleurs Des Mal, Mon Coeur Mis A Nu* would have long since vanished from the earth. Had Poe not become a notable figure through his tales and poems of the supernatural, I would surely not now be in possession of his *Marginalia*. And there can be little doubt that if Fernando Pessoa had not taken it upon himself to be the prophet of the rebirth of Portugal's age of glory, *Livro do Desassossego* would be now only food for worms. It is only celebrity status that impels our culture to preserve genuine expressions of the soul. This status need not be literary; it is enough if the writer is a famous athlete, actor, politician or criminal. Of course, one can hardly expect Marginalias or Books of Discontent from former stage or athletic entertainers.

There are occasional exceptions to this observation. Henry David Thoreau, the greatest inspirational force in American writing, became known only through the fortunate circumstance of his relationship with Emerson. Max Stirner's remarkable *Buch* gained attention because it appeared at a fortuitous moment in German history; a generation later, it would never have found a publisher, and in fact, almost completely disappeared after the events of 1848. But these are the rare exceptions; a literary work expressing the inner self is of no general interest except if it originates from a celebrity, thereby allowing it to gratify the insatiable voyeurism of the modern public. This is unfortunate because personal writings of this type are a means of connecting individuals–in my case is the only means of forming such connections.

Are there other writers out there who feel as I do?–who are concerned with their souls instead of their public? I have no way of knowing–perhaps it is better that I do not know. My task is my own development, a task quite large enough without my being preoccupied with a search for needles in haystacks.

Still, it would be pleasurable to find a living writer who says something meaningful to me in his writings.

* * *

The error of the 17th century philosophers was to conclude that God must exist because they could not conceive how consciousness could arise spontaneously. The error of 20th century scientists is to conclude consciousness cannot exist because they cannot conceive how it could arise from brain substance. These are examples of the arrogance of educated scholars who cannot tolerate leaving anything in a state of uncertainty. With all their hubris in other matters, the Greeks did not have this weakness. Socrates' most important contribution to Greek culture was to elevate uncertainty into a philosophical principle.

* * *

A question continually fascinating me is whether minimalism or maximalism is a better guide for self-expression. Is putting a whole philosophy into one sentence better than expanding it into a long treatise? Heraclitus or Hegel–who had the better style for objectivizing the soul? When this question is answered to my satisfaction, life will be greatly simplified for me.

* * *

Twenty-seven hundred years of western culture has produced a remarkable phenomenon of nature, the western individual. The bearer of this culture is a person whose consciousness is distinctive and recognizably different from other human beings. The tendency toward behavior *en masse* is found throughout nature at every level of animal development, up to and including the human. It is the emergence of individual consciousness that represents a new feature of existence, surpassing all spatial and temporal dimensions. *Being is thinking* for we humans. I have little patience and no interest for those who have not discovered this truth.

The important events in the world occur when a profound human being displays his thoughts in his writings. Thus I recognize the writings of Emerson, Thoreau, Kierkegaard, Nietzsche, to name some of my favorites, as monumental literary events, more than equivalent to the appearance of Napoleon, Bismarck, Lenin and Hitler upon the world political scene. Important literary events are major experiences in the lives of those attuned to human consciousness. The fact that individuals responsible for great literary events often become ossified symbols of their society makes it all the more necessary to penetrate beyond the symbolism in order to experience the substance of their writing.

One must overcome the widespread idea that literature is preserved for its own sake–not true at all, the justification for preservation of books is the opportunity to enter into the mind of their authors. This is quite different from mere exposure to interesting stories or clever essays.

* * *

There is enormous variability of my emotions and my consciousness. Like some kind of kaleidoscopic toy, they are changing constantly in every conceivable manner. It would be an impossible task for me to tabulate the number of things I have thought about, the emotions I have experienced and the varying opinions I have held in the past year, not to speak of a lifetime. Pessoa justified his pluralism of thought by stating that, like the universe, he too was plural.

However in one desire, I have never wavered no matter what the circumstances–the desire for the good and the avoidance of the bad with respect to my own inner being. I can never remember a time when I was not seeking to develop myself. When I feel this development is occurring, I am content with my lot in life, when I do not, I seek to change it at any cost.

* * *

The pervasiveness of the forces around me affecting my life is truly astonishing. I know that the influence of society is necessary for civilization to be maintained and that its members need to be directed in order to function as viable social beings. I understand that one must acquire the rudiments of civilized behavior, of culture, of skills necessary to survive in a complex society. I know all this but I cannot accept that there should be nothing else to my life. Something has to emerge as a consequence of all this training because it is impossible for me to imagine why one should be molded so carefully for so long merely to reproduce another person to be molded and so on and soon. What I perceive of value in the society is the independent spiritual nature of the individuals who compose it. If I cannot be an independent individual, then my life has been a failure and I would just as soon terminate earlier rather than later.

The gloomy thought will not leave me that an objective evaluation of my life reveals someone who is largely a creature of society–however I try to paper it over with the window dressings of my thoughts. What does my life really consist of? All kinds of affiliations, with a profession, with a family, with property, even with the fraternity of published authors. It is difficult for me to find any real manifestation of independence in my life other than the aspiration toward such a condition. But well into middle age, aspiration is not enough. Looking toward the future becomes ridiculous at my age; I have the feeling I am a habitual futurist, always rationalizing my lack of independence with the hope of future change. By being an independent individual, I mean acting out one's consciousness rather than according to innate instincts or societal training. Activities which have to do with money, fame or sensual pleasure (Spinoza's useful little triad of temptations), I do not consider as individualistic since they derive from socially engineered stimuli—regardless of how cleverly they may be decked out in a personal style. It is clear what I aspire toward even though I may not have achieved it to my satisfaction. The independence I conceive is not a matter of mere "freedom of choice" since this carries with it the opportunity to choose slavery which appears to be the choice of preference for most. Nor is it a matter of experience or knowledge since one may have experienced many things and know all that is to be known but still be a slave at heart. It is rather, so it seems to me, a matter of evolving one's consciousness *as a self-directive force*. I do not value any individuality deriving from outside forces of any type—even those which purport to foster individuality. No person or doctrine or circumstance can create my inner self; I have always found that when I attended to outside direction, I have ended weaker than when I began. My interest in the condition of the world is entirely a matter of curiosity, a most worthwhile motive, but the moment I allow myself to move beyond curiosity and become entangled, I am lessened and see my individuality weakened or nullified.

I desire individuality because I perceive it as the natural outcome of my nature. I desire to create my own soul because I perceive it as a superior reality transcending my physical self. No satisfactions bestowed by nature or society can compensate me for lack of a soul. Therefore, I desire to rise above nature and society. I am not content with a fashionable pseudosoul, I must have a real one, I must spiritually exist.

All these brave words do not deceive me. My spirit is willing but its forces are weak. Enchained by a hundred habits of mind and body, I continue on in the same old manner, fearful of new paths that would entail loss of customary securities. But I write in a new way; if I can give up the desire for literary recognition, anything is possible for me.

* * *

Obscurity is a great opportunity for the individual who knows how to use it. The problem is that most do not appreciate obscurity, thinking that if they do not receive some trifling piece of status from some paltry guild representative then life is cheating them out of some insignificant birthright. Such an attitude is understandable when it is a question of a livelihood but, more often than not, it is merely a matter of psychological needs. The deeply rooted instinct of humans to play out their life as a member of social groups is constantly interfering in the higher aspects of their lives. The social role creative artists perceive for themselves is to have an audience admiring their artwork. However, no one has yet discovered how to maintain spiritual independence while still aspiring for audience success with their work.

When I was younger, it was difficult to take myself seriously as a writer without having an audience. It was as if an arrow had penetrated into my heart when I first read Malcolm Cowley's definition that "A writer is someone with readers." At that time I did not fully realize the significance of the literary careerism of which Cowley was a leading representative. I desperately wanted to write but I felt ridiculous writing unless I had readers and thought the only way I could sustain myself as a writer was to achieve a modicum of literary recognition. I did not know my own importance without that crumb.

Recently, I read a book by Peter Sloterdijk (I cannot remember the title) discussing a return to the psychology of the Ptolemaic worldview after an era of Copernican scientism. Somewhere in one of my own works, I have made a similar observation but Sloterdijk has elaborated the idea in a most artful manner. Until I am capable of fully appreciating my position in the center of my universe, little of value can come from within me. An inspired figure once said that it is not what goes into a person but what comes out of him that counts. It is what comes out of me that counts, not my connections with an absurd American culture composed of tales of sound and fury signifying very little. I do not know what significance there is to my own life but I do know it has nothing to do with the opinions of strangers of whom I know nothing and care less.

All history, all culture, all civilization has culminated in the figure now seated at my writing table. It is necessary for me to fully assimilate the significance of this thought. There will be more than enough time to perform my tasks in the biological world in which I live; for now, I am my soul, center of the known universe, heir to all that the human race has been able to create, the last– perhaps the final–representative of that endangered species called *Homo sapiens*.

* * *

There is a certain charm and warmth to my literary life that would be certain to disappear were I to emerge from my snug nest of obscurity. Now I answer to no one and read or write to please myself alone. I have been a voracious reader through the years but I remember little of the works of the authors whom I have read. What I have read in the past is incorporated into the substance of my mind and is now part of me, no longer distinguishable from its origin. The important thing is that *I* have the thought, it is no longer important how I obtained it. The obscurity giving me a self-orientation as a literary person has served me well. When, out of the fullness of my spirit, I sit at my writing desk uninhibitedly pouring forth my thoughts and feelings, there is no thought of another to constrain my writing. What I am doing is confirming the reality of my inner self by transforming it into written language. Thus *I am*, not only because *I think*, but even more because *I write*. What greater fulfillment is there in life?

Everything hinges on the awareness of one's own soul. Without such awareness, my enterprise falls apart like a house of cards in a strong wind. When I think of myself as a creature of biology, merely flesh and blood, I am nothing except what the world thinks of me. I am a non-writer except as I have readers, I am a non-entity except as others think me to be someone. As a flesh and blood creature, the determinism of flesh and blood must rule. But once consciousness emerges, once I realize who I really am, it is what emerges forth from me that counts. I am free of the world.

There is no one raised in a western society who has not had his life deeply affected by Christian spirituality, flawed though it may be. The fact that I now live amidst only fossilized remains of Christianity does not negate the debt owed to it. As far as I can tell, the influence of Jesus of Nazareth as a human being quickly waned after his death and he became transformed into a cult figure. When Christianity disappears as a dominant dogma from our civilization, the full impact of this transformation will become evident. Meanwhile, I prefer to think of Jesus as someone I might have known, perhaps even as a kinsman, certainly as an inspired personality, if my life span had been inserted into his moment in history.

* * *

What do I owe to my culture?–to my society?–to my country? Only things in the material domain; I owe the debt incurred through utilizing the conveniences and products of the society within which I live. I owe society service that will recompense it for the space I occupy and facilities I utilize. I have no use for those persons who think they have rights within society without the obligation to repay it. If one does not pay society what is owed it, one has an obligation to retreat to a deserted place where one would not rely upon the services of society. However, I do not choose to take such a step, preferring to live within a social structure to which I contribute. This seems to me to be a more efficient arrangement for the conduct of life. In my own case, I provide medical services in exchange for the space I occupy and the products I receive. There might be some dispute over how much my services are worth and whether I am over-compensated but there is no argument regarding the basic principle. I work for what I get here.

However, moving into the metaphysical domain, everything is

different. Society has nothing to do with the state of my soul. It may be that has made it possible for me to have access to cultural influences–for which I have always paid–but it does not determine my reaction to these influences. Another person living exactly the same life as I have would never become what I have become. My interior activities such as sitting at this typewriter filling blank pages with my thoughts have no connection with me as a societal being. This is a matter between me and all existence; I recognize no role of society here. The fact that former arbiters of culture have made judgments which have affected my literary milieu is of no more relevance than the fact I utilize oxygen in the air I breathe or warm myself in the heat of the sun. The *Moirae* rule all that lives but one owes nothing to them anymore than one owes anything to the air or the sun for making life possible. All that is required of me with respect to my metaphysical being is that I become what I am capable of becoming.

Therefore I write for I have found no better way of developing my consciousness. I am not a "writer" in the vocational sense of the word because I do not desire to emotionally or intellectually stimulate readers. The esthetics of the written word has no value to me independently of its ability to bring forth and clarify the ideas in my mind. It is necessary that this be very clear to me since I have been so confused about it in the past.

To sum it up, there is no reason for me to write other than to create my metaphysical being. Otherwise, it would be just the same old entertainment game of which there are more than enough already in play. There is nothing more to say at this moment on the subject of my writing.

* * *

At one time, I thought that the essential element of consciousness was obtaining the experiences that generated it. I threw myself into a series of travels, relationships, adventures which appealed to me. I thought that I craved experiences when, in fact, it was really my inner self struggling toward consciousness. I learned that, in time, all experiences pall whereas consciousness never does and that experience is everywhere to be had at a moment's notice whereas consciousness requires something more, a certain redirection of the self from the animal state toward the human one.

* * *

Although it is quite evident to me at this moment that my inner being is a thing apart from my societal self, experience with life requires me to note that they both draw upon the same reservoir of energy so that drainage into one source depletes the other. When my brain has lost its strength, my consciousness will disappear. When the world is too much with me, I can do nothing except survive physically. If I work twelve hours daily, several days in a row, my inner being is extinguished. There are choices to be made and if I do not choose my inner self, it will disappear. If I permit myself to given over to another person, a career, a family, a cause, then nothing will become of the internal me. In the past, this internal me has been almost suffocated through such behaviors, so much so that I thought at one time the inner self was a delusions of mystics who were incapable of functioning in the "real world." Fortunately, I corrected that self-destructive error before it was too late. However, I paid a price through retardation of development so that it is only now that I am first confronting the essential problem of existence.

My first obligation is to the inner being I call my soul; this obligation takes precedence over every other one regardless of tastes, mores or vows. Society does not recognize vows made under duress or mental infirmity and I should not either. My primary task is to develop my inner being. This is what I must attend to through slow, prolonged deliberations and through the strength of resolve to follow the path marked out by them. Autodetermination– *Selbstüberwindung* to use a term from Nietzsche–is the key to success or failure as a human being.

＊ ＊ ＊

It is curious for me to note that the type of writings which now interest me are "passages" from diaries, letters or journals which have no grand architectural design. I no longer read novels or extended treatises of any type. In this I have reversed the habits of my youth when I was disdainful of writings less than full book length. I must also confess that I avoid reading English other than the daily newspaper, a vice that I have been unable to suppress. Since it has been years that I have read anything new in English of real interest to me, I have gradually developed a disinterest in my mother tongue. If I could write in a language other than English, I surely would. But I am grateful that I can read in several foreign languages that occasionally provide me with something of spiritual substance.

However, a price is to be paid for avoidance of one's native language. There is the tendency to *Selbsthass* that comes from the disdaining of something which is part of oneself. Fortunately, I reread Emerson and Thoreau regularly so I can bask in some rays of light from the English-writing world.

＊ ＊ ＊

Sometimes my strength fails me. . . . I am engulfed by a feeling of sadness so profound that it is as if my entire being has been swallowed up by a monstrous pessimism. Everything seems hopeless to me, bleak, without purpose or meaning. Where does this sadness come from?–I have no answer. There is nothing in my circumstances to account for it; I am in possession of my faculties, well-to-do, my health is good–yet I feel so without hope that it seems impossible that I should be any longer capable of further exertions on my own behalf.

My life feels then to me like a failure. All my youthful idealisms, all my aspirations for personal accomplishment, all my efforts toward making my life into something I could be proud of–all this has come to nothing and I find myself mired in a sea of petty affairs without the slightest sign that my real self, the inner me, has any impact on the outer world. No one knows that I exist. These writings I generate in moments of gloom are like messages in a bottle inserted by a solitary survivor on a remote island in an unknown ocean. I know they will never reach anyone but I continue to send them through some last despairing hope that someone will find me.

I have been betrayed by the world. I have done all that was expected of me and have found only sadness at the end of the day. Had anyone warned me in my youth that my reward for participation in glittering American society would be an old age of despair, I might have acted differently. However, fate did not wish me to be enlightened at an age when it could have counted. There are no phrases sadder than those containing the words "might have been."

No one knows that I exist. That is the core of the problem. What anyone whom I have any contact with wants of me has nothing to do with what I am. This is the source of my sadness—I am condemned to be an invisible man. The few shy gestures I have made toward revealing myself have been met by impatience, indifference or even hostility. My soul is shipwrecked on an uncharted island. As long as I ignore it and cover it over with the refuse of social life, I am able to maintain a shaky equilibrium. But it is becoming harder to keep my soul still, it cries out in its misery and sadness overwhelms me.

I have never found the society in which I would like to live and it is becoming increasingly apparent that I never will. Adaptation to solitude is absolutely necessary if I wish to live out my remaining years with dignity.

* * *

Contemporary fiction bores me. All these interminable stories as if the world has not had enough stories to last one an eternity. They appear in the same way as new automobile models; it is a necessity of the literature industry. Neither can I generate any interest in all the whyfors and howtos about what is up-to-date at the present time. They are all so many boring technical manuals as far as I am concerned. Literacy seems to be necessary to get on in the world but I see no benefits with respect to the soul–unless one breaks free of the current literature scene and can find a few wellsprings that have to do with the inner life.

The greatest amount of fresh energy in American literature today is to be found in poetry. But I must confess again that I cannot take poetical expression seriously. The devotion is to the form of expression, not to the consciousness behind it. Poets are always searching for the right word, the right phrase, the right rhythm–but what do such things mean? I, who am devoted to consciousness cannot take the language so seriously. It is only poets of exceptional genius who are able to maintain their devotion to thought at the same level as their devotion to language, and then one imagines how much more they might have said in prose. What a remarkable writer Shelley might have been if he had outlived his poetical inclination. Perhaps poetry is suitable for the young who need such a vehicle to give vent to their emotions but upon entering manhood, a different approach is necessary. A nation of children, however, will produce many poets.

* * *

For we human beings, existence consists of the universe and ourselves. There is nothing else. Since the universe I experience contains little of interest to me, I must necessarily turn to myself and face the facts without flinching. It seems evident that my self-centeredness, at least in part, derives from the banality of what is around me. I do not consider this to be a bad thing, bad morally or bad materially. If people were more interested in themselves and less in the world around them, we would not be confronted today by the destruction of the biosphere. Individuals who are interested in their own souls are not afflicted with the craze for consumerism which is destroying the earth. I have never had exclusive possession of an automobile. I ride a twenty year old bicycle and never buy anything new except under duress. My behavior does not derive from poverty or stinginess, it is a result of a mental orientation which does not generate interest in material possessions. If it were left to me, the entire insane consumer frenzy of the twentieth century would come to an abrupt halt–perhaps then there would be some possibility for the future survival of the human race.

* * *

I recognize that much of my reading is a kind of perverted "consumerism." Most often I read to evade the responsibility of thinking. Schopenhauer said in one of his immortal essays that reading is thinking with another person's brain. Of course, since I read that statement, I am somewhat in the predicament of the Cretan who said that all Cretans were liars. Nevertheless, the thought has germinated in my mind. My reading fulfills the definition of a vice; repetitive engagement in an activity to a degree which is detrimental to the individual. Reading is often detrimental to me in that it impedes the development of my own consciousness– which cannot be substituted for by the consciousness of any other individual. What was a mind-expanding activity in my youth has become a vice in my maturity. I should be thinking, not reading, writing, not reading, performing any kind of self-expressive activity but not reading.

Since I am incapable of totally abstaining from reading, I have been trying to limit it to a few areas and to only those writers who have something genuine to offer me. At this moment in time, I only read Fernando Pessoa and this partially to improve my Portuguese. I still learn from Pessoa in spite of the fact that I recognize much of what he has to say is *fado*—singing put into journal form. Like Thoreau in the nineteenth century, Pessoa has been an "event" in the twentieth century. What is really important for me, however, is to learn how to enlarge my consciousness and express it in my own way. I will not be satisfied until I feel I have achieved this goal. I must learn to *enjoy* the expression of my consciousness.

* * *

Again I am aware that my entire life has been an exercise in relating to the external world. Either I have been coping with it through acquiring techniques of living, or I have been seduced by it, habituating myself to its pleasures. I am virtually a total creature of my environment, whenever the environment is not stimulating, caressing or tranquilizing me, I have a vague sense of unease as though there were something amiss in my life.

Of course, I am not alone in my predicament. All around me, I see human creatures who are apparently incapable of existing independently in their surroundings. There is no capacity or desire for existing without a constant play of the world upon the senses. If it is not the chitchat of social intercourse, it is the attachment to computers, videos, radio, newspapers, books, magazines, cassettes– anything to escape the fearful problem of existing within one's own self. All kinds of empty homage is paid to the self but all I see are persons desperately looking for external means to relieve boredom or anxiety. No one really imagines that they possess a soul that can stand alone. The very term has become an anachronism and I read recently that young people no longer know what it signifies. They must have recourse to a dictionary to get the sense of the word's meaning.

Now I am not so unrealistic as to think a human being does not require interaction with his environment and society in order live. We are creatures of biology and are required, like other animals, to make an accommodation with our environment. Like all animals, we must eat, sleep and copulate at the proper times. We require protection from the adversities occasioned by nature and society, more the latter than the former. Furthermore, beyond our simple biological needs, our minds need exposure to the mental stimulation known as culture. Our emotions and imagination develops through this type of stimulation.

But something new must transpire at the end of this long process. There must appear an independent consciousness which is a new thing in the world, something which has not previously existed. There must occur the augmentation of being which is referred to as a soul. What does it mean to exist as a soul? It means that one has outgrown his dependence on the world for existence of his spiritual being. No one should delude himself that dependence on institutionalized myths or cults is an advance over dependence on parents. In the spiritual area, there exists only the soul–all the rest is biology or myth.

"I am that I am"–this definitive statement does not belong to the God of mythology but to the I which formulated it. Subjectivity is not objectivity, it is a new dimension in existence. Human life is destined to achieve it; those who do not move toward this destiny remain mired in an infantile condition or become prey to the terrible longings afflicting unfulfilled human life.

* * *.

Progress is the liberation of the individual from the blind forces of the universe that act to constrain him. As I see it, all life can be viewed as a liberation from physical forces which control inanimate matter. What is the difference between a rock and a living being except that the latter transcends the physical laws of nature. Life sets itself free from physics; something new enters the realm of being with the appearance of living substance. This can be seen from the simplest forms of plant life to the most complex mammalian species. It has always been known to thoughtful human beings that that survival requires overcoming the obliviousness of nature to their existence. Nature can only be appreciated after one has assured himself that he is no longer subject to its blind dictates. Anyone with common sense realizes he must cooperate with his society to achieve this end.

When I was younger, although I was aware of the significance of consciousness in my life, my appetites, i.e., the blind biological forces acting upon me, were too great for me to develop a position conducive to interior development. Although their manifestations were subtle, befitting the subtlety of the society in which I lived, my various drives and ambitions were nothing more than the usual sexual and survival instincts clothed in American social mores. It should not be necessary for me to recapitulate Freud. Nevertheless, I am grateful to have lived long enough to gain sufficient mastery over these instincts so as to provide scope for my position as a human being different from other animal species.

My status as a conscious being is dependent upon my ability to free myself from society. This is not a theoretical attitude on my part; it is the outcome of long experience that taught me society has not the slightest interest in my consciousness nor is it willing to extend the slightest encouragement to me to develop it. The most that I have ever obtained from those around me is a benign neglect of my yearnings in this area; the worst, an unconcealed hostile resentment. My investigations have led me to conclude that no one is ever valued by society for their consciousness alone. The exceptional historian Jacob Burckhardt once observed that nature only supports the species. Those who make their mark in society do so by participating in societal institutions or amusing the public, never by offering the inner self. Plato is known because he founded the Academy not because he wrote often boring dialogues.

The psyche is the product of millennia of evolutionary history in which humans have been conditioned to function as members of a society. I might as well tell myself not to feel sexual desires as to expect that thinking will liberate myself from societal influences. It is not likely that this will be ever possible, even when I have achieved control over most of my instinctual appetites. But it is enough to make a beginning, and to be conscious of the deleterious influence of society upon the spiritual self.

I do not have a great deal of patience with those who require belief in some kind of supreme deity or an after-life in order to develop their souls. This appears to me to be just another example of the hubris that afflicts my species. The fact that I am aware of something within myself which goes beyond the confines of physics and biology does not lead to a discovery of some kind of encompassing "All." "One world at a time" was the response of Thoreau to an impertinent questioner inquiring at his deathbed about his opinion as to an after-life. His attitude is the one I recommend. I really have no interest in any kind of "All" whether it be an Almighty or an All-Encompassing or an All-Pervasive. I do not believe that I am capable of such an extension of my consciousness. Most revelations of eternal powers seem to me to be techniques of mentally powerful individuals for dominating those who are less mentally powerful. The notion that a soul can be aligned with the mind of God is the utterest nonsense as far as I am concerned and results in the degradation of the intellectual conscience of those who persuade themselves of this dubious idea. Worse yet, it throws the whole intuition of the soul into disrepute.

One should be content to live out the energies of the self by expressing that degree of individuality one is capable of creating. After the moment in time of flowering of the self, what will be, will be. Not for one second do I think it has been given to me or any other mortal being to have a vision of eternity. Heraclitus long ago expressed the alpha and omega of all eschatological thought; "What is to come can be neither imagined or anticipated."

* * *

People need an historical sense. To quote Burckhardt again; "barbarism is the absence of a sense of the meaning of history." There is no other way by which the individual can evolve a consciousness of himself as both a member and a non-member of his society. Historical eras have their characteristics which dominate the life that goes on within them and invisibly influence the minds of the people who live during those times. For example, the antique world was dominated by the concept of *rationality* that emerged out of Greek culture. A person was judged by his ability to reason well and to affect others through persuasive rhetoric. Anything was acceptable as long as it was reasoned out carefully. It was not priests or generals who were admired most in the Greco-Roman world, it was the rhetoricians who knew how to use their reasoning power to sway the public.

Upon the advent of Christianity, the importance of rhetoric faded and *piety* became the dominant concept in the western world. One's devotion to the Christian way of life was the most highly admired human attribute. Whatever was done was required to be clothed in Christian piety in order to obtain acceptance. The brutal Crusaders and the greedy Conquistadors claimed to conquer the heathen world for love of Christ, not their own aggrandizement. This mentality persisted well into the modern era.

Now, however, we live in an age in which not rationality or piety, but *technology* is the most highly valued quality in society. This means that people most admire what works to control the material world. The *praxis* of the ancient Greeks, which was a lesser aspect of their culture, has become everything to modern western man. There may be lip service paid to beliefs or customs but it is the person who knows how to make things work who represents the highest ideal of our time. This is an essential insight for the contemporary individual to acquire. Society tolerates all kinds of beliefs and attitudes but what it admires is expertise in praxis. Anyone who is successful has an ability to *do* something apart from the rationality or piety of earlier times. Without a degree of praxis, no one in the modern world can ever develop a *modus vivendi* with his society.

The development of a *modus vivendi* with society, whatever its dominant characteristic, is not, however, the last word in human development. This is reserved for the process of human liberation from society so that a person may become more than a cog in a social structure. Just as what is ultimately required of a child is to learn how to stand free from his family, so what is required from an adult to stand free from his society. Today, it is not devotion to rhetoric or religion that stunts the inner growth of individuals, it is devotion to the material praxis of the modern world. Without this consciousness, it is impossible for the individual to become free of his society.

* * *

What is it that enters into forming the essential *me*? It is surely not the specifics of where I have been, what I have done, whom I have known–all of these things might have been different than they have been and yet my essential self still exist as it does at this moment. My sense of myself would be the same even though all the details of my past life were to be different. However, what I cannot envision is that I had not thought the thoughts that characterize my mind. *I am what I think* ; if I were to think other things, I would be a different me. The only way I have ever augmented my being and enlarged my interior self is through thinking new thoughts. Whatever has contributed to this thinking process has contributed to my augmentation; all else have been minor details. The worst thing I can do with my life is to dissipate it in activities which do not contribute to my thinking.

This must be the reason why I am averse to including the details of my daily life in these pages. These details do not contribute to my interior self; at best, they remind me of the boredom and inconsequentiality of most of what goes into everyday existence. The abstractions that are the life of the mind is the business to which I want to attend. Let others expound on the beauties of nature or the joys of love; I prefer the universe within me. I firmly believe that the greatest service the outside world has to offer me is some means of escaping from it.

* * *

It cannot be denied that there are gratifications associated with

REVERENCE FOR THE SOUL

attaining literary visibility. There is pleasure in being noticed for one's creative work, for rising above the anonymous individuals who create without recognition. It is human nature to wish to attain distinction in areas in which one endeavors to become productive. One need not dwell on the more obvious sources of pleasure such as royalty checks or literary prizes. These are pleasures toward which no one is insensitive, any more than one is insensitive toward culinary or erotic enjoyment.

The problem with literary success for writers is not the pleasures *per se* associated with it, it is that they distract them from the most important purpose of writing which is formation of the writer's soul. This has nothing to do with other persons, it is solely the affair of the inner self of the writer. Many professional writers who try to get at the matter of the souls do so after they have achieved success in the marketplace. But by then it is too late to write for themselves. They have swallowed the poison pill of writing for the public, something that is incompatible with writing for the self. A writer who expects a commercial publishing house to publish his work cannot shake free from the incubus of commercial expectations. Only a confirmed psychopath–which writers rarely are–can genuinely write for himself with the expectation of commercial publishing. Few writers are happy defrauding the purchasers of their products.

I believe the proper sequence for a writer is for him to first attend to the real business of serious writing as long as he feels himself capable of such work. After he has done what he can in the realm of self-development, he may one day wish to consider writing for the public. By then, his technical writing skills may be more highly developed putting him in a better position to be a "successful writer." At least, that is my notion of the sequence of development for a person who is drawn to writing. Socrates is said to have felt that writing was most suitable to the age of senescence when only memories were left to an individual but I am willing to concede a slightly earlier stage to be appropriate for public writing. As yet, however, I do not feel myself quite ready to become a public writer.

* * *

My little pile of sheets grows upon the writing table. As I type them, I am confirmed in my sense of myself as a recluse. There seems to be little literary innovation to my writings; the language is merely my blunt tool to express my thoughts. No one would ever be struck by originality in use of the written word. Mainly there is the effort to objectify the comings and goings of my mind and to stabilize the mental flux within me. I try to imagine what it would be like for another to read these sentences but the thought is disturbing to me; it is hard to imagine the motivation aside from maliciousness or voyeurism. Nevertheless, it occurs to me that if I were to be reading these words instead of writing them, they would interest me. I might sense a kindred spirit amidst a society in which I have never found one.

Of course, were I to be famous for some reason–were I a notorious criminal or politician or litterateur–then, no doubt, there would be many who would seize upon these writings as if they had discovered photos in the nude of a notorious actress. An editor once told me that I should become known, then my type of writings might sell–but fame would have to precede my entry into the literary world of the public. Fortunately for me, that has not occurred. I have a sense of serenity about my writing that would be lost if it were in my mind that they were destined for the public. To return to Socrates,–who is always a reliable source of wisdom in these types of matters–Plato has him advise against expression of one's energies in writing instead of in conversation. But writing for me is a kind of conversation, an interior conversation so to speak, without producing noise-polluting sound and providing a memoir for my future reminiscences. Socrates apparently preferred speaking to handsome young men rather than to himself. Not being attracted to homophilic activities, I find writing a more desirable method of self-expression.

* * *

No doubt many would condemn my literary life as narcissistic and lacking in the joys of human intercourse. I most certainly do not reject human intercourse, I only prefer not to involve it in my writings. Human intercourse is one thing, development of the soul is another. No one can make anything of himself who is preoccupied with the world of human intercourse. I find my society to be completely given over to human intercourse without the slightest evidence that personal interior development is being considered. I have never learned one thing about my soul from those around me. It is not surprising, therefore, that I do not look to others for my interior development.

I know that writing is necessary for my well-being because there are times, under the pressure of circumstances, when I do not write for weeks or months at a time. At such times, I am like a lost spirit, I am not conscious of myself. I become like one of these miniature trains that I see in the windows of toy stores that stop and start, go sideways or straight ahead, ring bells and light up, all at the command of an invisible engineer. At these times, my consciousness is replaced by an indefinable sense of unease, ultimately congealing into a contempt of self beyond my power of description. I plot various types of rebellion or insanity that result in the destruction of the entire apparatus; tracks, wires, machinery and trains. One may question my adjustment in life because such feelings arise within me, not to speak of my proven capacity to act upon them. But I have never found any means of permanently ridding myself of them. I do not believe that any permanent adjustment exists for a person like myself. Society is fundamentally hostile to the person that I am; any conception of my life purporting to believe otherwise is superficial and unaware of the realities of myself and the world.

* * *

I have sacrificed much to develop what I think of as my soul. Career, ambition, family, friends–all have been fed at varying times to the consuming fire of my desire for interior development. I have only maintained as much of my surface life as seems necessary to maintain the physical support for my self-development. Every time some path beckons to me that I think may lead me away from my main goal, I resolutely set myself against traversing it. Consequently, I am a non-entity to society, with no professional or business distinction, with virtually no friends, few family contacts and no discernable prospects for advancement in any of these areas. Least of all do I have literary success since I have refused to utilize what literary talents I have to cater to a market.

Others call me egocentric in the negative sense of the world. The fact is that I regard egocentricity as the highest good toward which humans can aspire. Egocentricity to me, however, is not orientation toward material ends but toward spiritual ones. Among the many lies that I have found prevalent in my society, the greatest one is that orientation toward others improves one's spiritual state. *Caritas*, at whatever level, seems to me to be of limited value since I do not believe one can ever know what is really good for others. The consequence of such an orientation is that both giver and receiver remain undeveloped creatures, looking for fulfillment without when they should be looking within. While "love," in its various manifestations, may have its place in the human condition, the individual who is immersed in this emotion will assuredly never develop his own self. Every self-respecting individual should pray to be saved from the unfortunate plight of anyone who loves or is loved unconditionally.

What does it mean to "develop one's soul?" It would be presumptuous of me to claim that I fully know the answer, I merely suggest that I have glimpsed its meaning. I imagine the ultimate development of the soul to be a condition in which one feels oneself to be equal to all eternity; nothing less will do. One must feel that the interior self is itself a universe equivalent, perhaps more than equivalent to everything external to it. The realization that the soul transcends physical being, transcends the universe of space and time, requires a special quality not easily achieved. If the individual possesses within himself the depth of consciousness to justify such a feeling then this is not the megalomania of brain disease, it is the megalopsyche admired in antiquity. The lunatic in an asylum noisily claiming that he is God is not to be believed merely on his own say so. But Henry David Thoreau writing "May I love and revere myself above all the gods that men have ever created" has a claim to credibility. It is failure to achieve this state that leads to desperation in those who are dimly aware of it. The human condition is such that there are many more desperates in the world than there are Thoreaus. I can exist as a desperate but the infantilism of "successful" people, believing Christians or the socially adapted is a state I cannot endure.

To develop one's soul means creation of a consciousness of one's self in relation to the world. The art of life consists in acquiring this consciousness. It cannot be a hobby or a diversion, like playing golf or doing crossword puzzles. It is a full time occupation, the one thing needful which superior individuals have always tried to accomplish. But few have had the purity of mind to will it unreservedly. Or if they do, they often trip themselves up, like Søren Kierkegaard, upon the loyalties of infantile attachments. There are no formulas for self-development, no gurus to lead one into consciousness, no progeny of God whose sufferings will redeem others, no leaders who possess a magic to bring others into fulfillment. There is only the desire, the egocentric will to achieve a better self. And above all, the absolute readiness to shed the swaddling clothes with which we are bound down by society.

* * *

As absurd as it sounds, honesty requires me to admit that only well past the midstage of my life, did I acquire the ability of truly thinking for myself. Although I have engaged in much reflection throughout my adult life, it was all reactive, merely changing from one societal formulation to another. Now for the first time, I have the feeling of being able to genuinely examine myself and my life, and to decide what is best for me.

I now have the good fortune of being able to meet my obligations through a type of work that does not drain my interior self. There is nothing so unfortunate as the plight of an individual who puts his heart and soul into work that gives nothing back to him in the way of interior development. T.S. Eliot suggested that the best occupation for a poet was a job with the post office. I do not mind giving over body and even the lower reaches of my mind to the service of my daily needs; I greatly resent, however, delivering all of my energies for such a purpose. It is necessary for me to have much mental leisure in order to perform the work necessary for my soul.

Thoreau claimed that he was able to support himself on the proceeds of six weeks of work per annum. But he did not live in the present industrial age, which has reduced his doctrine of simplicity in living to a shambles. As the complexity of life in our society intensifies, it becomes more and more difficult to live in it without mortgaging the soul. Most people I know have no conception of meaningful work that is not part of the money economy or does not provide some kind of tangible material benefit. There is general agreement on the message of society—the only work worth doing is that which pertains to one's material condition. There is some token volunteerism on the part of the wealthy or the retired but it rarely amounts to much.

Creative individuals throughout most of history were dependent upon some kind of support from a patron; more recently this type of support comes not from the rich but from a purchasing public. Best of all, however, is the creative person who depends on neither but creates purely out of the strength of self-reliance.

There are growing numbers of able-bodied and able-minded individuals who neither create nor work in any manner. They expect society to provide for them entirely on the strength of their status as human beings. They are the mirror images of the worker ants who support the social structure. These creatures are true parasites of society, however one wishes to explain the causes of their idleness. I allow others full freedom in what they wish to do with their lives; however, I am unwilling to give over any part of my carefully parcelled-out social labor to provide for those–or the offspring of those–who do not earn their living. The fact of being alive gives no one a right to make a claim on society and I do not endorse the blanket charities that my work supports. The first requirement of societal life is societal participation; evasion of this requirement through charity is destructive to both evaders of the requirement and providers of the charity.

Even this slight gesture at sociological thought leaves me exhausted and depressed.

* * *

Recently, I listened to a prominent Berkeley intellectual speak in public. A very suave, relaxed personality with rumpled jacket and suitably discolored jeans. He is well known as the author of a number of books best categorized as "New Age." I noticed quite a few of the members of his audience holding his latest book as they listened with rapt attention to his words. The room was filled to overflowing and many people had to stand in an outside hallway where they could hear his amplified voice without seeing him. I had arrived early but even so all the chairs were occupied requiring me to sit on the floor almost at his feet.

Although he was a perfectly pleasant type, delivering his remarks in an affable manner so that listening to him was something akin to sipping a chocolate malted drink, I nonetheless found a visceral sense of discomfort rising in me. After a while, the feeling was so strong that I could not remain in the room and left hurriedly when he was interrupted by a questioner. One could only describe my reaction to him as a feeling of revulsion. I tried to analyze the reason for this apparently irrational response. One might guess it was unconscious envy because I might have liked to have been in his position, handling himself so smoothly in public and receiving so much adulation. However, it is difficult for me to imagine that I could be envious since I would as soon be speaking publicly as I would be seated on a heated oven. I have more than enough experience in my life with public speaking and adulation. But what was it then that should have evoked my revulsion? As I have said, all his remarks were essentially harmless, fitting in with the prevalent "holistic" mentality; environmental concerns, health concerns, ethnic concerns, concern for the homeless, for the mentally ill, etcetera, etcetera. The usual Berkeley version of apple pie, motherhood and God. Perhaps his words might be the butt of some derision but no reason for revulsion. Surely he was a more appealing public personality than most of the politicians and professors that grace the public scene in my area of the country.

No, my visceral reaction to him must have arisen from sources other than the content of his remarks. For some reason, I remember a woman, perhaps in her forties, tanned and fit-looking, appearing to be mesmerized by the speaker, an intent look on her face as she clutched his book. It was something about the relationship of the audience to this man epitomized by this woman which revolted me rather than anything about himself. It was the appearance of so many well-educated, serious-minded individuals nurturing an illusion that this smooth-speaking celebrity was leading them toward a higher vision of the world, permitting them to share in a *Zeitgeist* that elevated their consciousness. It was Hegelianism adapted to twentieth century Berkeley in which the speaker charmed his audience into believing that he and they were celebrating a new world spirit, one which would make them better people and the world a better place. I did not see any better people, however, anymore than I saw better people at a Protestant revival or a Catholic mass. I only saw a crowd of children following a Pied Piper of a new age.

How could this kind of relationship of hero worship on one side and demagogery on the other, low key though it may have been, ever lead to elevation of anyone's consciousness? The speaker could not avoid manifesting a certain condescension toward his audience no matter how he tried to conceal it with democratic gestures. Conversely, no individual in the audience who permitted him or herself to be carried away by the speaker could escape the harmful consequence of submission to a charismatic personality. This person was doing the thinking for the audience; rather than the event being spiritually uplifting, it was spiritually degrading.

Some may think I am wrong in reacting with such a negative reaction. Listening to an intelligent, thoughtful person speak about issues of current concern–how could that be degrading? why is it necessary to be so negative?–a trait I have often been accused of possessing to an inordinate degree. Nevertheless, the situation appeared and still appears degrading to me. These people would have been better off at an athletic event in the Oakland Coliseum or at a cinema watching *Beverly Hills Cop*. Then they would not have been deluding themselves that they were participating in an uplifting experience. When one is charmed by a charismatic speaker appealing to current prejudices, carrying hidden self-serving agendas, ignoring the basic realities of existence and generally acting out of the ever present will to power of public personalities, then such an experience is necessarily degrading, not only for the people of the audience but also for the charismatic individual himself who cannot avoid his spirit being coarsened by these types of encounters.

To expect a successful author and speaker to uplift the soul is like expecting a neurologist to provide spiritual wisdom. The neurologist deals with diseases of the brain, the successful author and speaker deals with "edification" of the public. Neither can be expected to act as a guide for interior development.

* * *

I must confess feeling a certain envy toward those individuals who blithely feel themselves to be writing for posterity. That would be the best of all possible worlds; to be free of the constraints and irritations of celebrity status in one's lifetime and yet believe that fame and appreciation will occur posthumously when it cannot be harmful to the writer. But it seems incredible to me that there are serious writers who still imagine that they will be appreciated by posterity. From my vantage point, there has been a steady decline of the culture of western society–and today the whole world is western or wishes to be–so that it is most improbable that writers of spirit have much chance of exerting a significant influence in the years to come. European culture began its decline sometime after the seventeenth century with the result that our literary heroes are not the likes of Descartes, Spinoza or Leibniz but hordes of novelists, essayists and professors whose names are too numerous for singling out any specific ones. Societies can be judged by those whom they considered to be the best among them; thus one admires classical Athens, quattrocento Italy and seventeenth century northern Europe because of the caliber of men they deemed to be worthy of fame. Today it is entertainers and scientists who are lionized by our society, thus it is a mark of inferiority to be famous in the contemporary United States. Thoreau commented that he was born in Concord "in the nick of time," today no person of discernment could make such a statement wherever he might live. The more appropriate thought is that of Nicolai Berdyaev who perceived that a new Dark Ages was upon us, concealed underneath the illusion of scientific progress.

Thus it is foolish for the serious writer to maintain a hope that posterity might reward him with recognition. More than likely, each new generation in the foreseeable future will be more spiritually deteriorated than the preceding one. It is almost certain that the writings of truly spiritual individuals will find oblivion after their death. It is only the *present* to which the soul can devote its energies, it is only the *present* by which it is able to justify its existence, it is only the *present* that provides the reality upon which it can base its being because, for the soul, there is no temporal future.

* * *

Gradually I have discovered the root of a problem that has affected my writing. Underneath all my conscious thoughts to the contrary has been a stubborn yet unconscious feeling that somehow my writings should participate in a wider culture. It is as if it were not enough for me to create my own self through writing, I have swallowed the belief that it is also necessary that my work also has its place in some kind of cultural world process. This is what I have inherited from the Hegelian patrimony.

This inheritance has had a crippling effect upon me because of its inherent contradictions. Why should the development of my spiritual self be justified only in connection with a larger whole? What if this "larger whole" turns out to be a degraded phenomenon, less meaningful than what has come before and not worthy of my attentions? It is high time for me to fully apprehend and assimilate the insight that the individual stands above the group and that culture is at the service of the individual, not the reverse. I stand at the end of twenty-seven hundred years of western culture; it seems unlikely to me that the coming century will be an advance over what has come before. There is every evidence that western "culture," in the sense of spiritual development, is entering a period of retrogression. What I make of myself now is likely to be one of the last chances for some time for creating something of value within the human condition. I have paid various dues to society, it is not necessary that I pay cultural dues as well.

Once I emancipate myself from the thought that my writings must fit in to a literary culture, everything becomes much more fluid, much freer for me. Having broken mentally free from my attachments to family, religion and profession, breaking free of literary attachment seems to be a final step in liberation of myself as an individual. The circumstance which I perceive to be essential for human development is a *freely moving spirit* ; it is necessary to bend every effort to obtain such a condition. Immersion in a literary niche with all the impediments of expectant readers, profit-oriented publishers and the burden of literary celebrity makes it impossible for the spirit to freely move whether it be by writing or in any other manner. A kindly providence has protected me during my periods of greatest energy from the fate of literary bondage.

I have had to engage in the most monumental mental efforts to achieve what the philosophers of the antique world were capable of achieving with apparent relative ease. I am referring to the primacy of soul as set against the primacy of the institutions which bedevil human life. One can hardly peruse any extant antique literature without sensing that their authors took for granted the importance of the interior self in a way that is nonexistent in today's world. No one any longer takes his own soul seriously; the pervasive negation by current scientific beliefs of the reality of spirit has had its effect on the mentality of the times. Without the crutch of a mythologizing and paternalistic Christianity, people seem unable to take themselves seriously as beings with souls. Instead we have the materialist fixations of creatures living in a society where material possessions are the dominant reality.

It is better for me to have as little as possible to do with my society in the realm of spirit. It is enough that I have to abase myself in the everyday material affairs of life. In the realm of spirit, I have to protect myself from the ravages of the surrounding world. A man's spirit should be his castle; there in the safety of authentic being, he can construct what is of real value according to his lights. But for such construction to occur, the spirit must be absolutely free to move in all directions.

* * *

Every time I try to redirect my writing energies away from my own private work toward writing requiring an audience, there arises in me a resistance toward continuing the activity, no matter how apparently worthwhile the original attraction. I am as susceptible as anyone to the pleasure of creating something with a public impact. However, I find such pleasure not to be sustainable while that of private writing never palls upon me; rather the pleasure and sense of fulfillment continually increase as I become more accustomed to it. It seems as if I have become incapable of writing for the public. I am willing to engage in public service as a physician or citizen but not as a writer. Even the expression "writer" offends me; there is the ring of the paid professional to it. I consider myself to be a human being who writes.

Writing is my confrontation with the basic issues of existence. "What am I? . . . What should I do? . . . Where am I going?" These questions of Gauguin are what interest me and which I cannot put aside for lesser reasons. I value writing only insofar as it propels me toward resolution of these questions. There is little humor, narration or description in my prose; this is not because such writing does not have some appeal to me but because what motivates me to write is not concerned with humor, description or narration. There is more than enough of such writings in the world already, what is lacking is writing directed toward the metaphysical meaning of human existence, even more to the point, the metaphysical meaning of *my* existence. I feel there is something more to my life than material being; writing is the path I have chosen to find this something more.

Now is the moment allotted to me to develop my consciousness. After my death, the fate of my ideas and writings will be of no interest to me because I will be gone. The literary deification of dead writers and their writings generally have to do with the self-interest of professional literati, not with the significance of the writings. I would wish that the body of western literature were composed of writings quite different than those upon which literati have passed favorable judgement and, therefore, have survived. Much has passed into oblivion that would have been of interest to me. The survival of Fernando Pessoa's famous trunk crammed full of his writings unpublished in his lifetime demonstrates on what chance circumstances the preservation of writings depend. There must be thousands of unsung Miltons, thousands of trunks filled with significant writings that have never seen the light of day. But this is of no importance to their authors whose time on this earth has ended. What is important is that these individuals made something of themselves during their lifetime; no Platonic or Christian myths are needed to bring significance to the rise of consciousness. Consciousness is the intrinsic meaning of human life and it is the writer who has the best opportunity to bring this meaning into being.

* * *

I am inclined to believe that every person who is capable of doing so should compose his own epitaph to commemorate his death for those who might have been interested in his life. No one knows better than the person himself to what purpose his life has been directed and to what extent he may have succeeded in achieving it. This thought leads me to compose my own epitaph, since at fifty-eight years of age, the prospect of my demise cannot be considered to be far in the future.

EPITAPH BY HIMSELF

"He was a person who thought much about the meaning of human life, most of all, the meaning of his own life. These thoughts of his were often crowded aside by material preoccupations but as he grew older and more in control of himself, they became his closest companions. He believed in the metaphysical importance of his life and in bringing its meaning into his consciousness. There was little he would not do to acquire insight into his existence. He did not believe in a God or afterlife in the Judeo-Christian tradition so that all of his metaphysical desires came to be concentrated upon what he called his soul. Family, career and personal pleasures were subordinated to this one overriding preoccupation. Because of his way of life, his society came to think as little of him as he did of it; in time, he truly became a man without a society.

He had one personal relationship that mitigated his isolation; without it, he would not have been strong enough to survive. There is nothing left of him now except the memories of the few who knew him and the collection of books he read and writings he wrote. He had no illusions about the lasting qualities of these remains; he was at peace with the thought that he had had his chance to live the life he considered suitable for himself as *Homo sapiens*.

* * *

What I have achieved in my life has to do with negative as well as positive accomplishments. In this world of soul-destroying materialism, I have not fallen victim to the blights of careerism, consumerism or kin worship. Nor have I allowed myself to be entrapped by any of the brands of hypocritical religiosity that dot the American landscape like so many vultures perched on a decaying carcass. Avoiding these personal disasters has been as significant as any positive accomplishments to which I may lay claim. It is important for me to appreciate these negative accomplishments in order that I may maintain my morale in an environment doing everything possible to subvert it.

* * *

I note with amusement that, having moved from the worship of God to the worship of humanity, society is now moving toward the worship of nature. Thus we are moving full circle, reaching the stage that was the point of departure of antique culture. This attitude toward nature is an ideology, no different from ideologies about religion, race, nationality or political-economic systems. The beauties of nature lie entirely in the eye of the beholder. The ancient Greeks rarely note them, preferring to find their beauty in the human form or in architecture and artwork.

It should be clear to all who care to see that "nature" has no interest in the soul. What I see in nature is blind living, the swarming of species, incredible cruelty, an absence of all interior consciousness. The "natural" man proliferates in a manner analogous to bacteria, vegetation, rodents or any other type of living thing given over to natural laws. One need only roam through a virgin forest in which vegetation grows without restraint to see that overpopulation is not only a problem for animal species. The humanization of the planet with all its attendant menace to the individual is quite similar to unrestricted forestation and the swarming of insects, birds, fish, rabbits or any other living thing given a chance to overrun its environment. The way in which nature regulates these things can hardly represent a desirable model for those who have a sense of the worth of the individual of whatever species.

As far as I can tell, what is really valuable about nature is that it provides a means of escape from human society. I appreciate more than most finding some kind of natural refuge in which the presence of humans is not manifest. It is widely known that the human presence tends to ruin the possibility of appreciation of "nature." Conversely, if humans do not intrude on one's consciousness, pleasure and beauty can be found in most environments, whether they be "natural" or otherwise.

Fundamentally, nature is the scheme of existence into which we are born and in which we must find our place. Since I have had nothing to do with its creation nor desire to alter its configuration, there is little reason for me to generate a great deal of emotion or excitement about its presence. I would as soon go into rapture over oxygen in the air as over a sunset or a rainbow. Nature is not my affair, the center of my attention is an interior activity which has nothing to do with nature and, at best, exercises an uneasy truce with it in my body.

I have admired Henry Thoreau, not because of his fixation on nature, but in spite of it. Every genius is entitled to his idiosyncrasies.

* * *

Every person I have known, even the most mentally restricted, once they have established the basic groundwork required for survival, desire to move their lives onto a higher ground entailing more a more meaningful existence. There is no one who does not have this desire to go beyond simple biological activities. It must be because this wish is so prevalent that society provides a wide variety of *grooves* that permit individuals to believe they are participating in something more than the mere struggle for existence. The trouble with societal grooves is that, sooner or later, their direction is downward instead of upward. I have never been in a societal groove that does not at some point begin to conduct me in an opposite direction from which I originally intended to go. Whether it be a profession, a business, an avocation, whether it be family-oriented, society-oriented, profit-oriented–all societal grooves ultimately lead to a diminishment of the life of the individual. Those grooves, which at first are so reassuring and helpful in maintaining a steady course in one's conduct of life, become deeper and deeper, finally blocking out all vision of the real universe. They become so deep that one can no longer tell the direction of his movement, and if the forward course becomes easier, it is only because one is on a progressively downward descent.

Having recently emerged from my mental childhood, I prefer to avoid all grooves which are purported to make my progress easier. I choose to maintain my own balance albeit there are many times of unsteadiness and uncertainty of direction, even the possibility of a serious fall. Although I do not have the reassuring presence of firm walls on either side of me, neither is my vision of reality obstructed. I aspire toward the high ground of independently conceived existence. I must think out my life, it cannot be presented to me like some kind of secondary school curriculum. I was made to stand independently and this design must be fulfilled, however little I may be aware of its purpose.

* * *

INTERLUDE

Précis of a personal philosophy of the human condition. I recognize three stages in development of the individual; the biological, the socio-psychological and the metaphysical. At birth, there exists only a biological being, driven entirely by instinctual needs. Air, nourishment and protective warmth is all that is required by the newborn infant in order to be content. As it grows older, there are superimposed upon these basic needs the drive to explore the surrounding world and give vent to the emotions. These too are instinctual behaviors and occur without any conscious reflection on the part of the child. Later, sexuality is the last instinctual component to make its appearance and be incorporated into the repertoire of unlearned desires. Humans are no different from other mammals in their instinctual needs although their mental abilities refine their capacities for fulfilling them.

The socio-psychological stage of development is that which occupies most of waking life once humans emerge from the primitive nexus of instinctual existence. Social activity for a child is the *sine qua non* of its development in virtually every human culture. While a certain impetus to explore the physical world persists after infancy, the preponderance of the activity of the individual is funneled into social intercourse, whether it be with family, friends or representatives of societal institutions. Human development is difficult to conceive without social intercourse and one cannot imagine a child developing psychologically on a deserted island even if all its physical needs were met. The urge to form social groups is not merely an aspect of childhood, it pervades all aspects of adult life. One need only look about at the great variety of social interactions to realize how significant a force socialization is in human life. There is virtually no aspect of living that does not serve as a means for establishing social ties and providing a framework for the maintenance of social relationships. Just as a lattice fence serves as a structure upon which vines can grow and proliferate, so all the minor, inconsequential activities of humans serve as frameworks for the establishment of social bonds.

Social intercourse is so pervasive in human society that it is not surprising to find the view often expressed that it is only through human relationships that life is worthwhile. Aristotle, a moderate in most ways, expressed the view that without friends, no one would wish to live. It is evident that, although there may be some degree of material self-interest involved in maintaining certain social bonds, the principal element driving socialization is based upon psychological needs of the individual. Humans need interaction with others in order to feel psychologically healthy. All psychological therapies are founded on this phenomenon.

Most modern schemes of development end at the socio-psychological stage. However, I recognize a third stage that I call the metaphysical although one might with equal propriety designate it as the spiritual or consciousness-forming. It has to do with consciousness as an end in itself rather than merely as a means to gain the ends of earlier stages. The central fact of consciousness is that it cannot be analyzed according to prevailing scientific dogmas. It does not possess spatial existence, the cardinal feature of physical being. For this reason, it may be designated as a metaphysical phenomenon. Not withstanding modern myopias, there is no more reason for doubting consciousness as a human reality than there is in doubting one's physical or psychological existence.

Consciousness is most prominent in the individual freed from the preoccupations of biological and social affairs. It stands forth as the highest manifestation of human life; for this reason, the maxim "Know Thyself" was engraved in the Delphic temple and the "Kingdom of God" has been located in the human spirit.

The meaning of consciousness is an enigma to those who have concerned themselves with the study of the mind. When mental activity is directed toward physical survival or social interaction, the mind serves as a facilitator in the efforts toward accomplishment of specific goals. But consciousness as an end in itself is a uniquely human phenomenon unrelated to other goals. Consciousness as an end itself is a felt human need, comparable to other physical or social needs. It is directed toward all existence, physical and biological, and finally toward the conscious mind itself. No matter to what heights technology rises, it will never explain consciousness or even life because these are phenomena outside of the material realm of being. No matter how far the biochemist may track the beginnings of life down into curvatures of complex molecules, he will never, through the parameters of science, apprehend how these structures lead to the instinctual elements of life. No matter how deeply the neuroscientist may probe into the brain, he will never come forth with an explanation of human consciousness. The sooner our scientifically-minded society accepts that life and consciousness are forms of being existing beyond material methods of study, the sooner we may become again capable of engaging in the purpose of human life which is the metaphysical quest for consciousness.

Even more than life itself, consciousness is a transitory phenomenon when compared to the stability of physical being. There is no such thing as "consciousness" as a permanent state of being, there are only its kaleidoscopic features, forever in flux, like the surface of the sun. The "wise man" does not exist, rather there is the thinking person, always struggling to solidify consciousness but never absolutely able to do so. It is not possible to form a representation of the conscious mind because there is no image which will serve to represent it. The striving toward consciousness is a kind of Sisyphean task which no man would voluntarily assume if it did not represent the fundamental nature of *Homo sapiens*, the task he was born to undertake. The "virtue" of the ancient Greek philosophers, the "tranquillity" of the Buddhists, the "piety" of the Christians all represent different versions of the same awareness that a human being is destined to go beyond his animal being and societal self in order to attain, if only in a transitory manner, the unique condition called human consciousness.

Belief in God is a consequence of the human need to perceive something in the cosmos relevant to their own being. The remarkable durability of Christianity is the most compelling testimony to this need. Later, when the need to satisfy one's intellectual conscience became equally compelling in the scientific era of western civilization, belief in a benevolent God shifted toward belief in a benevolent Humanity. The concept that the individual could be part of the progress of all mankind was a satisfactory substitute to many for a belief in God. Spinoza's *Ethics* is the definitive statement, albeit in a virtually incomprehensible style, establishing the identity of belief in God and belief in humanity. For Spinoza, humanity represented an aspect of God, he conveniently merged the two concepts. During the nineteenth century, Ludwig Feuerbach put forth essentially the same notion with more emphasis on humanity and downplaying the idea of God. However, for Feuerbach and the armies of religious liberals who followed in his footsteps, the moral feelings formerly lavished upon the idea of a Deity were transferred to the idea of humanity. Finally, the religious trappings of Feuerbach were dropped entirely by the founders of scientific socialism who substituted for them practical material considerations. Higher wages were regarded as more important than enhancing spiritual development which came to be viewed as a myth propagated by capitalist reactionaries for the purpose of maintaining subjugation of the working classes.

Today, however, belief in humanity has gone the way of belief in God. Only the most naive or uninformed of individuals can still maintain belief in the progress of humanity. Humanity left to its own technological devices has produced over-populated, over-mechanized, over-polluted societies in which humans live in impersonal, frenetic and demoralizing conditions. An essential prerequisite (among many others) for maintaining the illusion of "progress" is the complete abandonment of the idea of the human soul. In past eras, the most important mark of the development of higher civilization was the emergence of awareness of the psyche or soul that distinguished humans from the rest of the animal kingdom. It was the psyche or soul that raised humans above the instinctual and stimulus-response activities of other animals. Consciousness of existence and freedom of action were the hallmarks of a spiritual creature. The Greeks thought only participants in Hellenic culture possessed this quality; barbarians were those people who did not possess a soul and consequently, lived an unconscious, unfree life.

All the evidence today is that "humanity" has reverted to the barbarism of the world that once surrounded Greek societies. True human progress would require reversal of this trend. Technology cannot replace the soul. Technological civilization does not recognize consciousness as a real phenomenon because it does not recognize the soul as a real entity. The only freedom that our society promotes is the freedom to become more deeply enmeshed in the materialist way of life. The absence of a significant awareness of soul is particularly striking in the English-speaking world where the term "soul" has become essentially a religious expression and only pertinent to the restricted area of religious discussion. There is no counterpart in the English language equivalent to the German word *geistig* referring to an intellectual-spiritual quality of mind.

In English, a person of "spirit" is enthusiastic, energetic perhaps but not anyone with interior depth. Nor does reference to "soul" improve the situation because in Anglo-American culture, as mentioned above, the term has little secular relevance. Gilbert Ryle, in his widely read and quoted treatise *The Concept of Mind*, firmly summarized the status of the soul in the English-speaking scholarly world; namely, that it does not exist. With the dominance of English culture in today's world, it is evident that other language worlds are following suit and the term "soul," outside of religious circles, is nothing more than a metaphor in whatever language it is written.

Consequently, the individual today with both a spiritual bent of mind and an intellectual conscience has nowhere to turn except to himself for fulfillment of his metaphysical needs. God and humanity are concepts of no use to him, it is only in his own individuality, in himself as a "thinking soul" that he can find the means to transcend animal existence. *Homo sapiens*, in the literal sense, no longer exists as part of society; if he is to survive, he must learn to do so in the solitude of his own individual existence.

* * *

PART II—A WILL TO KNOW

"Man is clearly made to think; in thought is all his dignity
and all his calling; and all his duty is to think as he should."

Pascal

Circumstances have brought me to live on the high plateaus of
the Navajo Indian Reservation. I am settled down for a time in
Kayenta which is one of the more arid areas of the reservation near
the Utah–Arizona boundary. The nearest cinema is seventy miles
away, there is no television reception and no bookstores within a
hundred mile radius. I derive much pleasure from these living
conditions. A half hour walk brings me into a world of canyons
and mesas, junipers and piñons, which is akin to visiting another
planet. All around me, desert nature is supreme, undisturbed by
the incursions of twentieth century technology and marketing. It
is not so much that the surroundings are beautiful and breathtaking
for there are many other areas that can surpass these canyons in
beauty. But here *I am alone* in elemental nature. There is nothing
to constrain my spirit, no restrictions on my movements, no noisy
multitudes, no competing activity to distract me. On top of a
high butte, looking miles in all directions with only the red earth,
gray rock and blue sky in my field of vision, my mind swells and I
become conscious of the reality of my being. I am free to think as
I can.

Spiritual space is as much a reality as natural space. Surrounded
by people and prohibitions, it is impossible to grow spiritually to

one's full potential. In the circumstances of desert living, one trades the stimuli of society for the open spaces. The reservation is a barren place, devoid of conveniences and modern "culture." I find the Navajo to be a quiet people, making far less impact on their milieu than the ambitious, aggressive whites who would quickly devour the reservation if U.S. law did not forbid it. There is spiritual space everywhere on the "res" for those who have the inner resources to utilize it.

Throughout the United States, the faculty of consciousness is abused by unremitting efforts at material achievement. It is necessary to periodically escape from this atmosphere in order to develop the inner self. Some type of arrangements are necessary to provide for basic needs–food, shelter, etc. The antique philosophers dealt with this problem by minimizing their needs to the utmost degree. The remarkable Greek Cynic movement was founded upon denying any reliance upon society in order to live and think. We take a different approach, basing our security upon insuring ourselves and our possessions. This is an expensive route to follow, requiring constant labor to provide such insurance for the modern, technologically-based life style. The reservation is an antidote to the proliferation of possessions and protections of American life. One realizes that it is possible to live without the enormous superstructure of "developed" societies.

* * *

Experience develops the soul . As much as the world changes, there are certain questions that remain the same for all societies, that have always arisen in all societies and will no doubt continue to arise as long as *Homo sapiens* continues to populate the earth. It is comforting to think that there are certain constants in the human condition which do not disappear in spite of the radical technological changes which ameliorate or afflict man's circumstances according to one's point of view. These are the spiritual or religious questions that come up in every life no matter how impoverished or wealthy the individual, no matter how prominent or obscure he may be in his society, no matter what his aspirations or his surroundings. These are the questions which have to do with his soul; there are no certainties when it comes to the soul and the individual has not yet been born who is assured with certainty of the well-being of his soul. There is a fundamental *Angst* which is the mark of the human condition irrespective of all other aspects of his life.

We live in a strange human world which has managed to convince itself that the soul does not exist, that there is only the brain and its appendages which serves to provide the phenomena that give rise to the illusion of a soul. My little treatise entitled *Souls Exist* elaborates on this curious aspect of the intellectual life of our society. Be that as it may, the fact that I should have been impelled to write such a work is an indication of the low esteem that the concept of the soul possesses at the present time. When there is a negative conception of the soul, then there is only a rudimentary awareness of the spiritual questions pertaining to it.

* * *

The hallmark of the soul is the consciousness that emanates from it. Pascal, a foremost representative of Christian thought, asserted that all human dignity consists in thought by which he meant an elevated consciousness. Christian consciousness is, of course, what he had in mind, but it is not necessary to subscribe to Christian dogmas to recognize the profundity of Pascal's central intuition. It is thought which makes the soul, it is thought which distinguishes the human species, it is thought which provides the individual with his essential reason for existence. Pascal, following the Christian faith, believed that the thoughts filling his mind were given to him by God's grace, a notion which has relieved devout Christians from carefully examining the origin of their ideas and beliefs.

The development of the soul needs to be the principal priority of every individual. As a member of society, there are other tasks which are placed upon him, he may have obligations to his family, profession or community. These are well-defined responsibilities in which the consequences of fulfillment are visible in the wellbeing of those among whom the individual lives. But the one obligation outweighing all the others is the development of his soul. One can overcome failure in all other aspects of existence but if one fails to develop his interior self–that is to say, his soul–one has failed in the principal task of his life.

How does one develop a soul? This is a question that has received remarkably little attention in western culture. In our scientific era, the idea of a soul has no currency and therefore does not receive the attention of the learned members of our society. Within the world of religious faith, ideas about the soul are fused with religious dogmas. Christians believe that if one finds Christ, all will be well with his soul. The concept of the soul is less developed in Eastern religions; there one is expected to find tranquillity rather than develop a soul. Among the rank and file of western society, it is assumed that conforming to the extant morality will result in a "good" person, one whose "soul" (whatever meaning is attached to this term) is in a proper condition.

But experience with life teaches otherwise. Those with religious faith may be mean-spirited, soulless individuals. Tranquillity may lead to a vacuousness of personality toward which few would aspire. Those whose behavior is proper in all regards may become either twisted or empty individuals in whom the concept of a soul is a mockery. There are no standards of behavior or belief that guarantee the growth of a soul. The great-souled people of the world develop their soul before giving allegiance to any particular faith or mode of behavior. How does this happen? Is there some secret in life which predisposes toward inner development?–another way of saying growth of the soul. If one is not content with the doctrine of grace, what alternatives present themselves?

Common sense provides a clue to the answers to these questions. It is obvious that a certain amount of contact with other humans, familial contact, societal contact, cultural contact, is required for an individual to acquire spiritual depth, i.e. to acquire a soul. There is no one I know, regardless of beliefs, who would think that a person raised in a closet could exhibit spiritual development. Even if such a person could survive physically, he would be an animal, a living being without human characteristics. Such examples have been found in children raised by animals or subject to extreme social deprivation from infancy. God's grace does not appear to ever been extended to such unfortunates.

* * *

The fact that individuals do not develop in the absence of significant social contact has been interpreted as indicating that higher function development is an extension of stimulus-response psychology. Modern psychology has grown out of the scientific tradition–thus it is monistic, materialist and non-spiritual in its orientation. The concept of soul has been long discarded in academic psychology serving as the training ground for most psychologists. A psychologist with a university degree may at times utilize the words "soul" or "spiritual" for the purpose of popularizing his writings but the meaning is only metaphorical–in his heart, he does not think these terms stand for anything real and may be embarrassed if they come to the attention of his peers.

There is no reason, however, for those who accept the reality of the non-material soul to be surprised that it does not develop in the absence of meaningful contact with other souls. If the body cannot develop without adequate nutrition, why should the soul develop without its own kind of spiritual nourishment? It is unreasonable to expect spiritual development to occur *de novo*, in the absence of significant and substantial stimulation from developed souls. The most spiritual individuals in the history of humanity, the Buddha, Socrates, Jesus, were all greatly affected by the spiritual thought of their times. Spiritual development requires contact with the spiritual substance of other souls; there is no such thing as *de novo* spirituality. Spontaneous generation is as impossible for the life of the soul as it is for the life of the body.

* * *

The hidden imperative in developing consciousness is experience. Without experience, there is no spiritual development. The significance of experiences is revealed by the intense desire of the young to acquire them. Travel, sports, learning, relationships, culture are the routes for obtaining the experiences that heighten one's consciousness. Fascination with psychedelic drugs is a manifestation of this desire. War has been the source of some of the most intense experiences available to humans although in the era of push-button technology, this experience like so many others is attenuated, not to speak of the immorality of wholesale push-button killing of others. The days of individual warriors and personal bravery have been submerged in the mechanization of human activity.

It is essential for the individual to provide himself with a range of broad, diverse and continuing experiences. The supposition that one obtains a repertoire of experiences in youth that serve for a lifetime (of societal servitude) is not in accord with spiritual needs. No one can ever have enough experiences, the problem in life is finding the ones which develop consciousness. One must constantly be on the hunt for meaningful new experiences. The spiritual imperative of expanding the mind requires risks to be taken in order to obtain them. More and more, however, rigidly controlled societies act to impede experiences, either by preventing them *in toto* or so diluting their impact that they have little value in spiritual development. More and more, the individual has to strive mightily to expose himself to significant experiences. Of course, one must remember that reading and assimilating a profound writing may be the greatest experience of a lifetime.

* * *

It is good to repeat, certain things need to said many times in many different ways. The fact that souls exist cannot be repeated too often in the contemporary climate of thought. The importance of spiritual development cannot be overemphasized. When one's soul is at stake, anything is justifiable in writing.

Many profoundly spiritual writers have chosen to present their thoughts in market-oriented writing. These are the professional writers with talent in story-telling or other literary genres that appeal to the public. Dostoevsky, D.H. Lawrence, Camus are a few of these who have become part of western culture. Even Kierkegaard represented himself as a poet and Nietzsche is regarded by critics as more of a prose stylist than an original thinker. If one needs to make a living by writing, he has to know how to keep the interest of a wide readership.

I have never been capable of being an entertaining writer. It is sufficient for me to express my thoughts as clearly as I can. Consequently, I do not have the excitement and gratifications of literary notoriety. But, in exchange, I have the pleasure of expressing myself in my own way without worrying about attracting readers. My faith lies in the intrinsic significance of self-development; if you ask me wherein lies this significance, I cannot give an exact answer but I trust my intuition.

The present writing is a continuation of a project of thought in which I have been occupied for much of my life. The project is my effort to track down the interior self and relate it to life experiences that have affected me. Writing down my thoughts is part of this project but by not means its entire extent. Schopenhauer has said there are three kinds of writers; those who think as they write, those who think before they write and those who do not think at all. I have never fallen into the last category but have oscillated between the first two. I have become persuaded that while thinking stimulates writing, the reverse is also true in that writing is an enormous energizer of my mind. However, Sartre's dictum of "not one day without a line" is an injunction for professional writers, not those for whom writing is part of their personal development. Writing too much is a fear that has been often in my mind.

* * *

Semantics is an important consideration for those who concern themselves with the interior self. Soul, spirit, self, mind, psyche, personality, consciousness, feelings, intuition are all words that have various connotations depending upon the background and education of the individual. People generally know what is meant by the self; the "I" behind all thought and feeling but will emphasize different aspects according to their interests. Intuition is distinguished from intelligence and spiritual being from cognitive self. Increasingly, the brain within the skull is the only reality accorded to the interior self as scientists believe all intuition and thought will one day be revealed as just so much electrical activity of neuronal circuits.

A recent book by Thomas Moore entitled *Care of the Soul* illustrates these semantic difficulties. The book is well written and filled with interesting experiences of the author who is trained in religion and Jungian psychotherapy. At the onset, the author states that it is impossible to define the soul. "Definition" he states, "is an intellectual enterprise anyway; the soul prefers to imagine." Later he distinguishes between "spirituality" and "soulfulness"; the latter is associated with emotion and imagination, the former with values and intellect. The author envisions the human soul to be distinct from thought; since he is true to his Jungian heritage, he values imagination and feeling above thought in the hierarchy of mental activities.

Differences in attitudes ultimately come down to differences in values. Moore's epigraph introducing his work comes from Keats, "I am certain of nothing but the holiness of the Heart's affections and the truth of Imagination." Consciousness and intellect are relegated to second place, if not considerably lower. This attitude reveals an anti-intellectualism that is a prevalent response to the scientific negation of belief in a soul. Imagination and feeling, however, is not what Pascal had in mind when he wrote that all human dignity consists in thinking. The dignity of thought has to do with thinking what is real not what is imaginary. One may derive pleasure from products of the imagination just as one does from playing games and one may appreciate emotions without which life is an arid affair. But what individuals want to commit themselves to are realities, wherever they may be found. Existence may precede essence, to quote Sartre again, but surely essence is a more important reality than existence. Thought is the essence of the human condition. We are "thinking reeds," to revert back once more to Pascal; a vapor, a drop suffices to kill us but we are superior to the entire universe by virtue of our consciousness of this fact. Whatever we care to call this capacity for consciousness–I prefer the term "soul"–it is where the dignity and calling of humans resides and to which our main attention should be directed.

* * *

The attitude of the author of *Care of the Soul* toward intellect and thought is certainly not unique among those interested in spiritual matters. The early Christians responded to the skepticism of the antique world by believing that God makes foolish the wisdom of the world and confounds its wise men. Secular philosophers have always been regarded with suspicion if not frank hostility by the established churches. With the Renaissance, however, came a rebirth of the role of the mind in society at large. A committed Christian like Pascal felt himself free to regard the life of the mind as the very essence of the human condition. The tendency toward suspicion of the mind today stems less from religious convictions than from a sense that the intellect has prostituted itself in the service of society. The developed intellect today is directed toward the mastery of nature rather than the rise of consciousness. This is nowhere more true than in American society where Thomas Edison and Henry Ford became the idols rather than Emerson or Thoreau.

The intellect is equated with know-how in professions and is expected to equip students to make money. Even philosophers, who now are only to be found as faculty in universities, pride themselves on being scientifically-minded and, as William James once put it, would wear white coats if they dared. They, least of all, have any interest in the intellect as a spiritual phenomenon.

Consequently, it is not surprising that thought has gotten a bad name and is no longer regarded by the spiritually inclined as containing all the dignity and calling of a man. But recourse to emotionality and imagination is no substitute for the duty of thinking fully and thinking well. What humans yearn for is reality; no substitutes will serve. Henry David Thoreau, some one who could hardly be accused of crass materialism, wrote "Be it life or death, we crave only reality." The consciousness we want is a consciousness of the reality of being. Whether it be of the reality of the universe and the living beings within it or the reality of our inner self, it is reality that is the key quality. The more our consciousness apprehends the reality of being, the more fulfilled we become. It is only the activity of the mind, our intellect, our thoughts, our intuition or whatever terms suit our taste, which gives rise to this reality. Myth and imagination may play a role in the processes of mental development but finally one must distinguish between them and reality else all is lost in humbug or illusion. We may not be able to live without coming to grips with our emotions just as we cannot live without coming to grips with our instincts, but this is no reason for abandoning the fundamental insight that recognizing reality is the first duty of a human being.

* * *

"Toute notre dignité consiste donc en la pensée. C'est de là qu'il faut nous relever et non de l'espace et de la durée, que nous ne saurions remplir. Travaillons donc à bien penser; voilà le principe de la morale."

It does one good to chew over Pascal, even if one doesn't swallow the polemicising on Christianity. To "bien penser," to think well, requires the objectivization of thought which is what the serious writer attempts to do. While one cannot fill space and time, the placing of one's thoughts within them is a noble substitute. No obvious purpose energizes this effort, it is the outcome of an indwelling urge defying analysis. Max Stirner said he wrote philosophy for the reason the little bird in a tree sings his song. It occurs to me that it is the *process* of objectivization of thought that elevates the thinker; what becomes of the product is a different matter, having to do with circumstances unrelated to the process. The growth of a thousand year-old sequoia has a significance in nature beyond its fate to serve as material for the ambitions of a subdeveloper.

Making something worthwhile of myself requires me to think well. No amount of success in the world at large through career, family, wealth or fame can substitute for thinking well. Even morality, as Pascal asserts, is founded upon profound thought and not supine reliance on societal standards. There are few more absurd creatures in this world than unthinking moralizers.

Penser–to think, to reflect, to value. Our era has persuaded itself that the soul is an epiphenomenon (more related to imagination than reality) and has defined thought as a cerebral process triggered by physical stimuli. The computer has become the model upon which is constructed a concept of the human mind, forgetting it was the mind that created the computer. Human dignity, however, does not lie in computer literacy but in the consciousness of all existence. Computers will become worthy to be ranked along side of human beings when they can communicate reflections and values independently of their programmers.

"*Bien penser.*" Words become clichés easily without representing the realities of existence. Thought today does not mean what it meant to Pascal, it is virtually entirely at the service of societally prescribed goals. Endless examples could be adduced to support this assertion which would be boring to enumerate. Emerson was the last American thinker of repute to preach consciousness of existence through high thought. American society ignored him and proceeded to subject thought to the service of high living and utilitarianism.

* * *

If it is utilitarian thought which forms the soul, thought entirely in the service of material existence, then this thought is a trivial thing, not worth the enormous effort of the ages which has gone into elevating human consciousness. Has all the spiritual labors of western history been for the purpose of providing automobiles for all or health insurance for the aged? The dignity and morality of thought is not the consequence of humanity on wheels or medicated bodies, albeit these may help to deal with the physical requirements of life. It is the dignity of the soul conscious of itself and of the nature of being as it is revealed to the senses. Who would not aspire to such dignity, once aware of its possibility?

The materialist world-view has deeply undermined the dignity of modern man. Physics and neurology has intimidated educated people into abandoning the instinctual belief in an incorporeal "I." Science is monistic and cannot tolerate the reality of multiple realms of being. The emergence of consciousness, however, represents an *augmentation of being* beyond material existence. No amount of scientific progress can replace this tendency within human beings.

The great merit of Kierkegaard was in never tiring of asserting subjectivity to be the distinctive human reality. The problem of semantics arises again; subjectivity did not mean to Kierkegaard what it means to a modern scientist or a Jungian therapist. Subjectivity for Kierkegaard was the Christian path to God (as it was to Pascal). One may have a different sense of the meaning of the path to God than Kierkegaard or Pascal without relinquishing the reality of the soul to which subjectivity refers. It is a matter of loosing the chains of an intellectually bankrupt monism that impedes spiritual augmentation of being.

* * *

One must learn how to deal with the monistic dogma that the soul is an "epiphenomenon" of the brain. Epiphenomena are beguiling things but do not partake of the reality of being. We need to think of the brain as an organ of transmission of thought rather than of its origin. One does not think that thoughts heard via telephone arise from the circuitry of the telephone itself. The brain is a natural telephone whereby it is possible for the interior consciousness to be transmitted to another although the transmission is always faulty and we know that no one knows another as he knows himself. We can as little conceive assemblies of neurons generating a unitary consciousness as we can imagine a finite universe or a beginning of time. And what cannot be conceived cannot be subject to dogma without violation of the intellectual conscience.

Human dignity is based upon the sense of self as a thinking being. Scientific reductionism has no place in this phenomenon. Success in society is a significant experience but in itself does not lead to deepening of the sense of self. Failure in external life is perhaps more important than success for the soul's development. In the free choice of life's experiences and the inclination to reflect upon them lies the true art of human life. Without freedom of experience and leisure for reflection, nothing is spiritually possible. It is necessary to reverse the scriptural injunction; it is from freedom— and reflection—that truth arises. Freedom and reflection, however, can be difficult to sustain.

* * *

My Writings. The project of thought I am pursuing is a continuation of a theme dating from 1980; my published writings are

Affirmations of Reality (1982), *Philosophical Artwork* (1983), *Fanatic of the Mind* (1987), *Souls Exist* (1989), and several collections of aphorisms, some of which were put in graphic form. It is seven years since a writing of mine was last published although I have never ceased recording my thoughts. When I leaf through the aforementioned works, I have difficulty recreating the state of mind that led to their composition. I was then capable of such fine phraseology, such astute commentary, such clear intuitions. My present self seems puny and inarticulate compared to the writer of the Eighties. It is hard for me to recognize the identity of the man I was then and the person who sits at my writing desk today. Perhaps I should let well enough alone and not tamper with what may have been better done in the past.

Yet I am still alive, still attempting to discover the reality behind my daily life. Goethe's Faust says it well in the oft-quoted phrase:

> "Nur der verdient sich Freiheit wie das Leben, der taglich sie
> erobern muss."

which I translate as "freedom as well as life are earned only by those who must win them daily." The individual who wishes to maintain his freedom and his life must constantly overcome the annihilation that threatens the human spirit at every stage of its existence. It is only through constant thought and action that a life worth living can be obtained.

The theme I still pursue has not changed however. It has to do with the affirmation of reality, an expression I utilized for my first writing and which might well be the title of all my works, merely adding numerals to designate their sequence. The issue revolves around definition, meaning and significance of the word "reality." The naïve conception of reality, namely material being which is the prevalent notion, cannot seem worthy of serious consideration to anyone who has thought deeply about the human condition and has explored the thoughts of those who have expressed themselves on the subject. It seems incredible to me, two centuries after Kant, that the average person still thinks the "real world" is what exists outside of him in the surrounding *materia*. It is one thing to have instinctual reactions, it is another to have a philosophy of life based upon immature ideas. The greatest treasure one can have is a concept of life based upon the realities of being. And, as Scripture says, where your treasure is, there will be your heart also.

* * *

A human being cannot achieve his destiny as long as he is bound to the naive conception of life exemplified in childhood. For a child, the outside world is everything, the "inner self" exists only in incipient form. As a person matures, this situation changes, he develops an interior self which is something more than mere will or instinct. Historically, this interior self has been referred to as the "soul" although so naming it does not mean it is a spatial entity like the organs of the body. Perhaps it would have been better to have followed the lead of the ancient Hebrews with respect to naming God, specifically, to abstain from the practice of naming or, when absolutely necessary, to use only initials. JHVH is less likely to be desecrated in discourse than Jehovah, God or Lord. Perhaps instead of using terms such as soul, interior self, spirit, personality, etc., we should use only letters, e.g. SL to refer to the incorporeal being that is part of human life. Then it would be clearer that one is dealing with an entity not subject to the laws of materiality.

Be all that as it may, this writing expresses one man's conceptions about the nature and relationships of "SL." It presupposes a mystical sense, an orientation beyond that of mechanics and chemistry in responding to the phenomena of existence. Human development, throughout the ages, has been dependent upon a mystical sense; when this is absent or present in a debased form, great misfortunes have fallen upon all involved.

* * *

Brief Ontogeny. From the beginning of life, humans reveal their desire to explore the world around them. Infants exhibit the most remarkable curiosity about objects in their environment and wish to handle and taste everything they see. As soon as they develop the use of their legs, they wish to explore the world in the most fearless manner, sometimes leading to disastrous consequences if their guardians are not vigilant. However, they are not only interested in the physical world, they are also interested in sounds and words as evidenced by their uncanny ability to learn the language spoken around them. Curiosity and the desire to learn are the hallmarks of the human condition at all ages. It is not without cause that Aristotle introduced his *Metaphysics* with the famous assertion, "All men by nature desire to know." The "desire to know," without reference to utility, is the predominant characteristic of *Homo sapiens*.

What is it exactly that human beings want to know? They want to find out about the real world but as individuals grow older, it becomes more difficult to discover exactly where the real world is located. The childish interest in surrounding objects gives way to an interest in the meaning of things that is more difficult to uncover. There is a great deal of falseness and deception in human society that frustrates those who maintain their interest in discovering the real world. Gradually, the interest in "knowing" gives way to an interest in "possessing" since it is easier to possess something than to understand it. But, in the long run, possession does not meet the fundamental needs of a human being as does knowledge and the person who reaches old age with many possessions but little knowledge becomes an object of pity and derision.

Learning how to walk, talk and read are great accomplishments in the course of human development but they are only the beginning of a long process of humanization. The critical phase in the development of maturity has to do with acquiring an awareness that the reality all men seek has its locus within the self rather than the object world. This is not to say that the reality of the object world does have its place in human affairs but that it is subordinate to the reality of self just as locomotion does not lose its importance after the individual learns to speak, read and write. It is a matter of hierarchy of development. And, of course, the most recently acquired capacities are those which are the most susceptible to go awry or not develop at all.

* * *

The orientation to self has historically been most often associated with a religious consciousness. The discovery of the spiritual self becomes associated with an assumed greater spiritual being–the concept of God. Christianity and the Hindu-Buddhist traditions have connected the awareness of the inner spiritual self with the idea of God. The mystical wing of all churches has always justified their existence by claiming their inner discoveries to be the work of their God. Thus the discovery of self has been for a long time identified with religious revelation. Intuitive knowledge and sensory experiences were often intimately fused by religious mystics.

It was the landmark accomplishment of Immanuel Kant in the *Critique of Pure Reason* to make clear to those who could read it that reality was to be known only in a limited way via the facts of sensation. Through the most carefully thought-out examination of sense experience, Kant demonstrated that the spatial and temporal framework in which we imagine external objects to exist and the causal relationship which they exhibit with one another is entirely a function of the way we think about things as distinguished from the real nature of these things–which Kant believed to be unknowable. We accept the information of the senses–the so-called phenomena from the Greek word for appearances–because it is instinctual and convenient for us to do so. It provides the basis for our survival as living beings. But as far as revealing the reality of the world around us, the phenomena have only limited value and are deceptive when it comes to understanding the real nature of existence.

A

The conceptions of Kant are difficult to grasp just as any developments past childish ideas are often not easy to comprehend. Most of the superstructure of organized religions are founded upon the belief that spiritual understanding is difficult to acquire. People are more comfortable with the familiar object world of childhood than they are with Kantian concepts. Most are not willing to do as recommended by the apostle Paul, to put away childish things in order to think as a man. At the basis of the failure to develop a sense of the spiritual self is not perverseness but laziness and ignorance. This is the Socratic notion abandoned by Christianity in favor of the idea of sin. However, laziness and ignorance are well known human traits while the idea of original sin seems implausible and is based upon a far-fetched Old Testament myth.

* * *

Whatever the reason, it is indubitable that people have difficulty recognizing that more reality exists within their own selves than in the surrounding object world. This failure in mental development is not merely an inability to acquire some abstruse philosophical concept. It is more serious than that, it is a failure to recognize wherein reality lies. The consequence is that, consciously or no, persons who have not a sense of their own reality put their energies into the object world because that is where they think reality is to be found. One might say the tragedy of human life is the failure to recognize and explore the reality of self. Perhaps this is overdramatizing, perhaps a more accurate view is that nature is profligate with human life and is willing to allow much of it wither in an undeveloped state for the sake of the rare fully developed flower. This was the Nietzschean viewpoint. Time will tell whether the human race is destined to move *en masse* beyond the cognitive style of its animal origins.

During the tidal wave of scientific and technological development in the nineteenth and twentieth centuries that followed the Kantian era, the ideas of Kant were relegated to the dustbins of academic philosophy because they had seeming little relevance to the "real" world being uncovered by legions of technologically-minded investigators. But with the passage of time, it has become evident that scientific investigation has only a limited capacity to reveal the real world. What science can do is tell its devotees how to control nature but can do little to elucidate the realities of the natural world. Life, the cosmos, the inner nature of the physical world–all these recede tantalizingly into the darkness the more scientists, with their endless array of instruments, try to penetrate their essential being. An enormous amount of human resources and energy are expended in descriptive science and in the construction of bigger and better mousetraps to corral nature. The human "desire to know," however, is unsatisfied by pyramid building and more and more is directed toward other avenues of understanding. The efflorescence of interest in myths, superstitions, native cultures as well as in traditional religions reveals the widespread need to learn something beyond what is offered by science. It is not likely, though, that the refurbishment of beliefs dating from earlier stages of societal development can satisfy for very long the "desire to know." One can lapse back into childhood for brief periods but there is no permanent return to naïve world views for societies which have known the powers afforded by modern science.

* * *

The prevailing *Weltanschauung* is that of "scientific monism." Even those who may never have heard of the term still subscribe to its dictates. Scientific monism may be characterized as the point of view believing that there is only one type of existent substance; namely, *matter*. All the combinations and permutations of the world are capable of being reduced to the matter of which the world is composed. This matter is subject to scientific investigation. The phenomena which have not yet been explained by physics and chemistry will one day be so explained; it is only a matter [sic] of time before such mysterious things such as life or mind are rendered understandable by scientific study. There may be fringe elements that resist this viewpoint but they exert relatively little influence on society as a whole. In general, it appears to be true that the more affluent and successful a society is, the more likely it is to be dominated by the concept of scientific monism.

Why is science so strong? Why has the attitude of scientific monism been so strongly implanted on the modern mind? In my opinion, it is because of a hidden factor concealed behind the facade of the objectivity of science, a factor that has a long history of exerting powerful influences in human affairs. I am referring to the phenomenon of *magical thinking* that underlies a great deal of human behavior. Modern science, behind its facade of dispassionate objectivity, feeds upon the human tendency to ascribe magical powers to those who know how to manipulate nature. Science is magic which works. Throughout recorded history, the capacity to heal disease, to predict future events, to create over-powering machines have been associated with magical powers in the eyes of a public susceptible to such things. Modern science, with its enormous panoply of instrumentation capable of peering into and controlling natural processes, has inherited the cloak of supernatural power formerly accorded to magicians, shamans or high priests. Thus the mindset of the public is not that science is merely a method for obtaining limited results in a circumscribed area but that it is a means for divining the mysteries of existence. There seems to be an inexhaustible faith that, in time, science will know all things and solve all problems.

* * *

The "desire to know" which is the predominant characteristic of *Homo sapiens* is channeled within societies according to prevalent societal attitudes. Thus, in the antique world of Hellenism, the study of philosophy was the principal vehicle for discovering the nature of reality. With the coming of the Christian era, institutionalized Christianity replaced the antique schools of philosophy as the repository of knowledge of the real world. With the coming of the Renaissance and the emergence of scientific pioneers such as Galileo, Copernicus and Newton, science replaced religion as the guiding light to the knowledge of reality. Institutionalized religion has not disappeared in the wake of the triumphs of science just as antique philosophy did not completely disappear subsequent to the hegemony of Christianity. Parenthetically, it may be noted that the era of science has been kinder to religion than Christianity was to its predecessors. Nevertheless, there can be little doubt where the dominant concepts originate in the world of the twentieth century; they are to be found in the teachings of materialistic, monistic, institutionalized science.

* * *

The "desire to know" is the dominant instinct in the human mind. It has so evolved as to rise above the primitive instincts of personal survival and reproductive activity. The "superior person," *Der Übermensch* of Nietzsche, is someone in whom this instinct has reached full flowering of expression. Another way of expressing this idea is to say that enlarging consciousness is the goal of the superior person. Consciousness of what? one might ask. Consciousness of all things pertaining to the human condition is the answer.

The question arises from whence arises this desire for consciousness. There are those who have pointed to the snake in the Garden of Eden. Others imply it comes from a Higher Consciousness pointing us in the right direction. These ideas have no substantive meaning. When it comes right down to realities, we humans know nothing and can know nothing of a supposed God, neither his thoughts nor his will; all reports that impute otherwise are fallacious. There are some things that are beyond the ken of human knowledge—the origin of the desire for consciousness is, I believe, one of these things. Another is the existence of God, another is the question of immortality. There are others that arise periodically.

Whatever its origin, I like to think there is a spiritual continuum occupied by gleaming points of consciousness representing human minds. In its totality, these represent a pointillistic canvas that forms a profounder cosmos than that described by the physicists and astronomers. Every conscious human being can be proud to be a part of this cosmic creativity and should strive to gleam as brightly as nature has made possible for him.

The greatest barrier to the formation of ideas which enlarge consciousness are other ideas impeding mental activity. Some ideas are like computer viruses that spread throughout the mind and inhibit its ability to engage in independent thought. The idea that the "will of God" has been revealed to individuals or churches is one of the most pernicious of these ideas. The amount of damage done to human mental development through the belief that revealed wisdom resides in religious institutions has been incalculable. A person who has been indoctrinated with religious dogma during childhood is someone who has been crippled for higher mental development. He may overcome the indoctrination by a supreme act of will but the signs of crippling will remain forever.

On the other hand, the contemporary cynicism and delight in the absurd particularly to be found in scientific and academic circles is contemptible. A mature person without some value beyond his own or his family's needs is someone who has not achieved full mental stature. *Homo sapiens* is meant to evolve a value system based upon his consciousness of the spiritual element of existence– if this does not occur, there is something wrong with the way he has lived his life.

Religious dogmatism and scientific materialism are the Scylla and Charybdis through which the frail bark of the contemporary human condition must find its way without shipwreck. Circes there are aplenty to mislead the gullible navigator.

* * *

Friedrich Nietzsche–a man with an inspired mind but a flawed physiology. His concept of "Ubermensch" pointed to the direction humanity needs to take. The translation into English as "superman" is ridiculous, reminiscent of a comic strip character. Walter Kaufmann's translation as "overman" is no better and meaningless to English readers. "Superior person" is the closest English can come to Nietzsche's meaning.

Like the virtuous man of the Stoics who could never be found, Nietzsche's Ubermensch does not exist in the contemporary world. Certainly it is not Nietzsche, perhaps not any philosopher since Socrates, not any literary or political figure in recorded history. Yet it remains the worthiest ideal of recent times. Unfortunately, the representatives of humanity I am familiar with seem to be receding from rather than moving toward this ideal. The witches' brew of scientific technology, global capitalism and socialistic government is not producing superior people; rather the reverse seems to be the case. The "self" has disappeared as a philosophic concept. Since the neurosciences have been unable to localize the self in the brain, it is presumed that it does not exist. Consequently, pharmacology, neurophysiology and evolutionary theory are the principal contributers to the understanding of the human phenomenon. Psyche-ology is no longer of interest except to superannuated theologians and a few archaic eccentrics.

However, reality is still a force in human affairs. If there is such a thing as the "self," if it is not accessible to the reductionism of modern science, if its substance consists of something other than neural membranes, dendritic synapses or neurotransmitters, if, in fact, Descartes was righter than the swarm of career-seeking materialists who followed in his wake, then the sages of science will have to change course in order to achieve that one thing which humans desire above all else–the knowledge of reality.

Somewhere, Thoreau has written that what he desired above all other things was a *realometer* to tell him when he was on the right track toward reality. Regrettably, science has not produced such an instrument and there is a great deal of off course activity in human affairs. Yet it is still possible to change direction—all that is needed is the will to do so and a sense of reverence for the human soul.

* * *

The struggle of the intellectuals of the 18th and 19th centuries in western society was to break loose from the rigid embrace of institutionalized Christianity. This was accomplished and those who wish to express themselves freely can do so without fear of physical harm. However, religious dogmatism has been replaced by a more subtle yet more oppressive force, that of scientific monism. The human spirit is denied because it is not accessible to scientific study. Such is the prestige of science that its consignment of the "self" to the realm of nonreality carries great weight with all those educated to regard science as the ultimate arbiter of all truth—just as it was difficult to deny Christian superstitions two centuries ago. The weapon of science is not persecution, it is reliance on its mastery over natural processes and disregard of all that does not follow its materialist dicta. In the long run, these are more potent weapons than persecution.

The only really original thinker of national repute to appear in the United States since Emerson and Thoreau has been Robinson Jeffers. He received the same treatment as did Thomas Paine a century earlier when he defied the national ethos. His ideas were vilified, he himself was viciously attacked and his reputation destroyed. Now at a safe distance of years, he has been adopted by the usual literary chic who cluster around individuals of fame regardless of their beliefs. Jeffers understood the meaning of the term "truth" and was willing to stake all on expression of his beliefs. Were he alive today, his writings would be no less vitriolic as "truth" has even less status now then in his time. Young men may not be sent now to their death in dubious wars but their minds are being destroyed by a soulless education and spiritless values.

* * *

Having overcome the tyranny of established religion, western society has now been seduced by the powers of science. Science is magic organized on an unheard of scale; this sums up the entire matter. There is no end in sight as legions of busy scientists continue to produce new feats which enable humans to feel ever more powerful in relation to nature. Science is magic because the laws of nature, upon which all scientific technology depend, are a mystery as far as the how and why of these laws are concerned. The ultimate particles of physics have disappeared in a haze of unpredictability. The laws of gravity can be described but not understood. The origin and nature of life remains an enigma because nothing biologists have learned explains the movement toward what Teilhard de Chardin called the continuous *complexification* of species. Darwinism does not explain the philosophic mind. And finally, no scientist has been capable of envisioning how neural activity is transformed into consciousness. All that is known is that when the brain is altered, consciousness may be altered also. But, as William James pointed out a century ago, how one leads to the other is a great mystery.

A price is paid by individuals who are preoccupied with magical activities. There occurs a neglect of self leading to the loss of the basis of human superiority; the consciousness unique to humans. People are like nations, when they put their energies into exploiting their milieu, they weaken themselves and are ultimately worse off than they were before the exploitation. So it was with the imperial nations of the world and so it will be with societies dependent upon scientific exploitation instead of development of the self. In time, people will become like ants, consciousness will atrophy away and the human species will give way to some better form of life.

* * *

It is popular in certain circles today to explain consciousness as a biological development with survival value for the human species. But why does life strive to maintain itself by means of ever more complex forms of existence? Surely simplicity has more potential for survival than complexity. Why did not life evolve through unicellular diversity that would have been a more effective and less problematic system for the maintenance of life? Darwinism explains how species evolved but not why they should have evolved into increasingly complex forms. This is the task of metaphysics that has no instruments at its disposal, relying solely on the power of the developed mind.

Evolution seems to have changed course from physical development toward consciousness development. But there are obstacles, the most prominent being the persistence of obsolete religions and the idolatry of scientific monism.

* * *

There is an oracular tendency dwelling within me. When I try to stand back and look at myself objectively, I appear absurd to myself, perhaps even pathological. I am a prophet without hearers, a general without an army, a teacher without students, a writer without readers. Yet the instinct is too strong in me to deny so I must assume there is some significance to it. It is my consciousness expressing itself—the one act of real meaning in human life. Max Stirner said he philosophized for the same reason birds chirped their songs in the treetops. For that metaphor alone, Stirner deserves to be remembered.

I have never learned anything of real value from my elders, my teachers or my contemporaries . . . anyone whom I have known in the flesh. Much was taught to me about how to be successful in my society (at which I have proven at best to be a mediocre student) but nothing I consider to be of enduring significance. That has only come from within myself or from things I have read which is why I put a high value on literary activities. But I can count on one hand, two at most, those writers who have taught me something that sticks to my bones. Seneca, Thoreau, Nietzsche, Pessoa come to mind immediately; perhaps a few others could be mentioned. Christian writers such as Pascal, Kierkegaard, Berdyaev and Teilhard de Chardin have bemused me for long periods of time but in the end, their allegiance to Christianity undermined their value to me. If there is a weakness in the foundations of someone's thought, the ultimate structure does not stand the test of time for one who values intellectual integrity.

* * *

It is not surprising that belief in the existence of the "self" (soul) is being destroyed by scientists and their camp followers. The self is an incorporeal phenomenon; all the efforts of modern technology have failed to give evidence of its existence. The modern world treasures technology above all else so it is to be expected that the self is not included in scientific formulations of reality. What isn't measurable doesn't exist.

The computer craze sweeping society as the twenty-first century approaches is one more example of the inanity of scientific endeavor in our times. Minds are dominated by the constantly changing requirements of computer technology; more than ever, "things are in the saddle and ride mankind." What is the good of all this information processing and reprocessing? The individual already has vastly more "information" than he can profitably utilize for his self-development. The obsessive lusting for more and more appears to be a sign of group madness such as that seen during the Crusades or the Third Reich. Increasingly, the material element of life is overcoming the interior life. But who cares for the interior life?—a myth according to our contemporary paladins of science, a vestige of the superstitions that once dominated mankind. It is this refusal to perceive the spiritual nature of man that will be the downfall of our society.

* * *

Christianity has been the principal vehicle of spiritual development in the western world. Its value for this end has been severely limited for a long time–as Heine said more than a century ago, "The great Judeo-Christian God Jehovah is terminally ill with no hope of recovery." Nietzsche pronounced him dead not long after. As a consequence, piety is replaced by entertainment in the churches, faith has become a hollow shell with little evidence of interior commitment except for groups of fanatical fundamentalists.

Why has Christianity become a spiritually moribund institution for the individual with an intellectual conscience? Some reasons may be proposed:

1. Conversion of the remarkable but mythic personality Jesus into an object of idol worship.
2. Requirement for belief in unbelievable events.
3. Regarding the legends and homilies of the Bible as the "word of God."
4. Reliance on priests, ministers and charismatic preachers for guidance in spiritual development.

None of the above is new but the power of inertia in human affairs necessitates constant repetition of things that need saying.

* * *

Consciousness has the same relationship to the brain as the sun has to the solar substances undergoing combustion. Every thoughtful person knows that analyzing solar energetics does not do justice to the phenomenon of the sun. Something eludes the chemists—how did the process begin in the first place? What is its meaning in the cosmic scheme? From whence came such vast quantities of energy? One cannot ignore these questions and still think to explain the phenomenon of the sun. Similarly, consciousness is not explicable by means of strict confinement to the neural sciences. Something more is needed.

One learns more about consciousness by investigating the experiences that produce it than the organ with which it is associated. Consciousness derives from life's experiences; a person locked in a room throughout his life does not acquire a consciousness worthy of the name. Here is my list of experiences that may (but not necessarily) lead to consciousness. Others might produce a different list.

1. Experience of emotions. One might justifiably state without experiencing the passions of life, there is no real consciousness of existence.

2. Experience of beauty. Dostoevsky said in one of his novels that beauty will save the world. He was preoccupied with the power of female beauty but there are many forms of beauty perceivable in the cosmos; nature, animal forms, human art and so forth.

3. Experience of superior minds. However, it may occur, access to the interior world of others is the single greatest impetus to interior development. One recognizes a model that can be used toward this end.

4. Expression of self. Not knowledge of self but expression of self should have been the oracle of the Delphic priestess. The luminous image of Socrates transmitted through the millennia comes from his expressive personality. All genuine artists and writers know that creative expression–expression of self–is the royal road to personal development.

Consciousness signifies energy. Like the flames of the sun, it is in constant movement, enlarging or contracting, intensifying or fading. The absence of interior development indicates senescence and death. If there is a God in the scheme of things, he must manifest himself in the dynamism of human consciousness.

* * *

For a while, we can live off the spiritual capital of eras that sustained belief in the existence of the soul, but in time, the implacable conviction that we are exclusively material beings will radically alter our way of life and thought. The conception that the whole dignity of mankind lies in thought cannot be transposed to neuronal arrays and dendritic networks. Consciousness of self, that is to say of one's values, feelings and visions will inevitably be discarded as relics of a superstitious era. If the mind is nothing but a biological computer, if consciousness is nothing but an epiphenomenon of neural processes evolved to further gene survival, then ultimately barbarism will be restored parading as progress and the beauty and dignity lying behind the facade of the world will disappear.

Where then is truth? Are the paladins of science right? Is everything above only sentimental nonsense designed to perversely impede progress? Like Socrates' *daimon*, my intuition tells me no. In a civilization and culture totally created by the mind of man, man is still the measure of all things. Human consciousness that emerged on the world stage during the evolution of mankind is not the product of scientists and is not discernable through their peculiar instruments. Self-consciousness deserves to be put ahead of science and profound thoughts ahead of its instruments. Science is here to serve human consciousness by defining and controlling its environment; if its minions pass beyond this role, they must be taken in hand, admonished and ridiculed if necessary. Samuel Butler's lost society of *Erewhon* provided the ultimate solution to the tyranny of science–prohibit all new machines!

Joseph Wood Krutch arrives at the heart of the matter in his *Human Nature and the Human Condition* (1970):

> "We cannot now 'control the machine' because we are hypnotized by it; because we really do not want to control it. And we do not want to control it because in our hearts we believe it more interesting, more wonderful, more admirable, and more rich in potentialities than are we ourselves. We cannot break the hypnosis, cannot wake from our submissive dream, without retracing one by one the steps which brought us more and more completely under its spell."

This hypnosis must be broken if *Homo sapiens* is to be worthy of fulfilling the "divine drama of the universe" to which allusion has been made.

* * *

"Ideas Have Consequences." The legacy of Albert Schweitzer is very much alive in western culture. Schweitzer's concept of *"Ehrfurcht vor Leben"* –reverence for life—is the dominant morality of our times. Schweitzer meant human life but one can find this concept extended to all forms of animal life in the sect of Brahmanism that condemns taking any animal life down to the tiniest insect. Vegetable life seems to be excluded from the prohibition– presumably even Hindu saints must eat something.

This type of morality has become linked to the medical-industrial complex with some very bizarre consequences. The phenomenon is now widespread of human carcasses of all ages being kept alive through use of tubes inserted in numerous orifices and blood vessels. These carcasses may be without sign of animal life; no movement, no speech, no signs of mental activity. But reverence for life–backed up by dogmatic life preservationists–keeps them alive. The compassionate deaths accorded to domestic animals and livestock are denied to human beings. Discussion of such matters is a taboo subject for professionals involved with the care of the debilitated and the dying, and it is a felony offense to help someone exit from a pointless life no matter how grim their prospects may be.

The antique philosophers believed that one of the cardinal elements of wisdom was knowing when life was no longer worth living and acting on this knowledge. Now billions are spent on care, medicine and procedures designed to keep decaying bodies alive regardless of the nature of their life. Women are told it is immoral to terminate their pregnancy whatever the effect it will have on the woman's future life. The mindless lump of protoplasm growing in a uterus is accorded the same "reverence"–and legal rights–as any fully developed person participating in society.

I say it is reverence for the mind rather than reverence for life which should enter into the moral consciousness of human beings. Decay and death are as necessary as bad weather; it is as ludicrous to interfere with these processes through technology as it would be to interfere with the weather. Nature certainly does not "revere life," why should we humans, who are attempting to do more than merely live, erect the preservation of life as a categorical imperative. The divine drama of the universe is not fulfilled in every DNA-bearing piece of protoplasm, it is fulfilled in the individual consciousness of a thinking, striving human being. Let us only revere that which is truly worthy of reverence.

* * *

I have recently read *Promethean Fire* (1983) by C.J. Lumsden and E.O. Wilson in which it is asserted that "for the first time since William James examined such old fashioned notions at the turn of the century, research on the innermost processes of reflection and feeling have become fully respectable."

Not respectable in my mind or in the mind of anyone who has carefully read James' discussions in his epochal *Principles of Psychology*. None of the problems raised by James regarding the identification of brain with mind are even considered in the current neurobiology era, much less resolved. They are merely ignored and it is accepted as an article of faith that mind is an information processing device consisting of nerve cells instead of silicon chips. None of these blithe researchers concern themselves with how cellular activity becomes a higher consciousness or how the unity of self is subserved by millions of individually firing neurons. Because the answers to such questions cannot be found (James could not conceive of any monistic answers), modern biology, and with it, modern culture, is abandoning the concept of "mind" as a unitary entity. In its place is substituted the notion of mind as an information-processing device in which nerve cells act as silicon chips. It is classic scientific reductionism in which a simple paradigm that is understood is substituted for a highly complex phenomenon which is not. But the mind exists as an entity transcending nerve cells and if ignored, will make its presence known in forceful ways. To paraphrase a metaphor of Nicolai Berdyaev, the subsoil of modern scientific culture is volcanic and will erupt sooner or later with consequences unforseen by the advocates of psychobiological materialism.

* * *

The progress of the human species has been founded on one thing and one thing alone, the development of consciousness. Religious or scientific dogmas that stand in the way of full recognition of this truth impede human development. The great scientific discoverers of the past who have enlarged our understanding of the milieu in which life exists and develops; Copernicus, Newton, Darwin, Sherrington, Einstein, to name a few, have always avoided the hubris of imagining their theories could be extended to include that which created them. Twentieth century researchers into the human condition, beginning with Freud, have been more arrogant and have extended their reach to everything in sight–and to the phenomenon of mind. But the lesson of human culture, of which science is a subset, does not support the endeavor. Science has no intellectual basis at the present time for reductionist explanations of consciousness, it has working for it only the enormous prestige associated with its technology. This prestige and the power associated with it has been frightening for a long time to those with the vision to see beyond technology. The Victorian writer George Gissing penned the following prior to two World Wars when there was less disaffection with modern technology than there is at present–attesting to the profundity of Gissing's insight:

"I wonder whether there are many men who have the same feeling with regard to "science" as I have? It is something more than a prejudice; often it takes the form of a dread, almost a terror. Even those branches of science which are concerned with things that interest me–which deal with plants and animals and heaven

of stars–even these I cannot contemplate without uneasiness, a
spiritual disaffection; new discoveries, new theories, however they
engage my intelligence, soon weary me, and in some way depress.
When it comes to the other kinds of science–the sciences blatant
and ubiquitous–the science by which men become millionaires–I
am possessed with an angry hostility, a resentful apprehension.
This was born in me, no doubt; I cannot trace it to circumstances
of my life, or to any particular moment of my mental growth. My
boyish delight in Carlyle doubtless nourished the temper, but did
not Carlyle so delight me because of what was already in my mind?
I remember, as a lad, looking at complicated machinery with a
shrinking uneasiness which, of course, I did not understand; I
remember the sort of disturbed contemptuousness with which, in
my time of "examinations," I dismissed "science papers." It is
intelligible enough to me, now, that unformed fear: the ground of
my antipathy has grown clear enough. I hate and fear "science"
because of my conviction that, for a long time to come if not forever,
it will be the remorseless enemy of mankind. I see it destroying all
simplicity and gentleness of life, all the beauty of the world; I see
it restoring barbarism under a mask of civilization; I see it darkening
men's minds and hardening their hearts: I see it bringing a time of
vast conflicts, which will pale into insignificance "the thousand
wars of old," and, as likely as not, will whelm all the laborious
advances of mankind in blood-drenched chaos."

The Private Papers of Henry Ryecroft

Today, we may doubt that Gissing (a.k.a. Henry Ryecroft)
was born with an anti-scientific bent of mind but that it was
generated by his growing up during the efflorescence of industrial
England to which was added his own extraordinary prescience.

* * *

Currently, it is in fashion to regard mind-brain identity to be
supported by the Darwinism. Biologists have decided that the
mind and its ideas evolve in the same way as do lungs, heart and

kidneys and can be subjected to the same type of research methodology. Culture is in the process of being biologized. The mind, however, is a different category of being than are lungs, heart or kidneys and needs a different approach for its elucidation. Great minds operating in the realm of ideas are needed to ascertain human realities; microscopes and electrode implants are of little use. And least useful of all is the construction of mechanical imitations of the human brain which lack its essential attributes. One is reminded of the story by Heine about a mechanical robot created by a clever Englishman which, in spite of being able to do all that humans do, spent its time ceaselessly roaming the roads of Europe, asking every bypasser how he could acquire a soul. No one could ever help him in his quest.

Much is made of social relationships and social communication but we know others principally through our organs of sensation which are, by definition, organs which function through physical processes. Our ability to intuit the spirit of others is wholly dependent upon our own spiritual development; without this development, the consciousness of other souls is a closed book. Therefore, attention to self is the *sine qua non* of meaningful interpersonal exchanges. Let no one think this development can be contracted out–not to entertainers, professors, priests or the Lord himself in heaven. No one can do for a person what needs to be done by himself.

* * *

"Only in individual consciousness is fulfilled the divine drama of the universe."

Antero de Quental

This vision is hard to maintain; Antero took his own life not so long after writing the lines from which this quote has been taken. Society does not encourage participation in divine dramas. A considerable dose of contempt is needed to shield the soul from defilement and destruction. I have noticed with dismay that most of my literary heroes died by their fiftieth year.

Writing for me is an extension of my consciousness. By formalizing and objectifying my thoughts, I provide my mind with a stability and direction that is not present when vague ideas merely rattle about in it. I feel that I honor my thoughts by giving them an independent existence to the best of my ability. If some other person finds them to their liking or helpful, all well and good. But as Thoreau observed, we come into the world not chiefly to make it a better place but to live in it, be it good or bad. I make no promises to any readers regarding my thoughts; perhaps they will find them boring, irritating or even detrimental. No matter, I have performed my sacrament, all will be well regardless of the fate of my writing.

Pessoa was once asked in what direction his development as a writer had progressed through the years. His answer, now famous, was; "I don't develop, I travel." So it is how I perceive myself as a writer. When I read things I have written in the past, it is often as though they come from a different person, there is some resemblance to my present being but also a great difference as though I were speaking a different language. Who is to say that I am "developing," perhaps I have retrogressed from my previous condition. I am only sure that I am speaking from different places. The important point is to live and think and express the inner self wherever one may be in point of time.

Attempting to analyze my own writing, I note it is impossible for me to follow an outline or a fixed schedule—so many words per day, so many pages per month, completing chapter by chapter according to a prearranged schedule. This is the method of the professional author who is preparing work for the entertainment or edification of the reading public. Year after year, even decade after decade, this author follows his system and may amass a huge literary opus.

My method is different. I can only write for as long as the internal pressure within me demands expression; once it is relieved, nothing more is forthcoming. If I do not write for prolonged periods, however, and ignore the need to do so, something in me withers and I become another kind of person whom my writing self does not recognize. But I must live and think as well as write, and I cannot do all things simultaneously. The divine drama of the universe is not easy to perform.

* * *

For a long time, I have had the premonition that humanity—at least the humanity I have experienced—has gone awry. It is not technology which is at fault, not the superannuated religions that refuse to fade away, nor is it the absence of God in the minds of men; it is none of these things, it is the fact that the individuals have become bewitched by the machines they have created; they are intoxicated with the powers they think machines have bestowed upon them. The inner being grows less and less significant, more and more, all pleasure derives from mechanizing existence. Between us and the world of insects increasingly lie only differences of size and ingenuity.

   This will not go on forever; it is consciousness, not mechanization, which is the denouement of the cosmic drama. Humanity can be replaced; how or when is beyond my ken. I don't have the inclination to cry, "Repent, repent," society is driven by its inner dynamic beyond my reach. I don't intend to go the route of Nietzsche driving himself mad from undertaking tasks beyond human capacities. A miracle is needed—or a catastrophe.

* * *

Things Which Give Me Pleasure. Coffee with M., walking my dog, reading books which inspire me. A glass of wine before dinner, a night out in our tent under the stars, a trail through unsullied nature far from the sound of people. Putting my thoughts down on a few pages of white paper. Browsing through my library.

I am no longer able to read novels. While I can watch a good story at the cinema or on television, my expectation from books is higher. I must encounter the spirit of the writer or else my interest wanes. It appears to me to be a shame that intelligent, talented individuals have to divert their energies into storytelling instead of self-assertion. But I know most writers have to earn their livelihood. I thank providence that I am free from that burden as far as my writing is concerned.

When Socrates was asked how he could live with Xantippe, a notorious shrew, he responded that learning to live with her gave him the experience necessary to manage mankind at large. This is how I feel about living in America; if my soul can survive life in the very crucible of technology gone mad, where *Bildung* means becoming computer literate, then there is nothing in this wide world beyond me.

I note with approval the saying of Samuel Johnson that the difference between the lettered and the unlettered was as the difference between the living and the dead. One must, however, understand the meaning of the term "lettered." It means someone who knows what and why to read and prefers his letters to the machinery of the world.

The final end for all education (I refer to real education, not vocational training) is to become conversant with the thoughts and personality of great individuals. This requires concomitant development of one's own mind that may greatly delay the educational process. In my own case, my development has been so slow that it has not been until the approach of old age that I feel myself truly conversant with a few great minds.

* * *

Reverence for soul is the credo which I advocate to all those who want to make something of themselves during their allotted life span. It requires, however, determination and a great deal of nay-saying to society.

The seducers of humanity in the past have been theologians .
. . then psychologists . . . now the biologists are moving to center
stage with biobabble about genes, culture and human kinship with
all living creatures. I don't deny I may have descended from apes,
amoebae and what else but it is what my mind is now and can
become which concerns me, not my ancestral history. All these
scientists really should learn their place in human affairs. But people
will say or do anything for career and pocketbook.

* * *

End quote for educators:

> "These disquisitions will probably seem dry and useless to
> such readers as are accustomed to consider only sensible
> objects. The employment of the mind on things purely
> intellectual is to most men irksome, whereas the sensitive
> powers, by constant use, acquire strength. Hence, the objects
> of sense more forcibly affect us and are too often counted
> the chief good. For these things, men fight, cheat and
> scramble. Therefore, in order to tame mankind and
> introduce a sense of virtue, the best human means is to
> exercise their understanding, to give them a glimpse of
> another world, superior to the sensible, and while they take
> pains to cherish and maintain the animal life, to teach them
> not to neglect the intellectual."
>
> George Berkeley

All the current emphasis on instrumental learning is merely a
more refined way of saying that it is Bishop Berkeley's "sensitive
powers" which count. Never mind thinking too much, expand your
information-gathering capacities; never mind exercising judgement
and discrimination, your helpful programmer has done that for you.
And don't be preoccupied by ultimate questions that make no money;
all that has already been worked out by the doctors of technology.

* * *

I believe that expressive writing, more than any other activity, is the ultimate human experience. When an individual has objectified his consciousness in a literary work, he does not need reviews, cameras or microphones to trumpet his accomplishment throughout the world. He has transformed his interior self into an "oeuvre" which is the most significant thing one can expect to do during his brief life span. He has realized the end of what all social progress is supposed to be the means—the emergence of the consciousness of *Homo sapiens*. What use may be made of this activity by others is a secondary and lesser question. One can safely leave it to an all-knowing providence.

PART III—
REVERING MY
SOUL

What is noble? What does the word "noble" mean today?
The noble soul has reverence for itself.

Nietzsche

Human beings are metaphysical animals. In spite of all their remarkable abilities to analyze and control nature, there is within them an unquenchable urge to go beyond the phenomenal in order to discover the inner nature of things. The capacities of humans, however, appear to be far more developed in the area of analysis and control of nature than in that of metaphysics. For this reason, the analyses of natural phenomena, otherwise known as "science," are far ahead of comprehension of the inner realities which fall into the category of "metaphysics." There are light years separating modern science and its technological attachments from the accomplishments of antiquity in this area; however, regarding metaphysics, the antique philosophers stand head and shoulders above their modern successors.

Because science has so far outstripped metaphysics, the belief has emerged among educated individuals that the metaphysical urge in humans is a primitive relic destined to be largely eradicated by the discoveries of modern science. Any stubborn core of metaphysical need that persists is supposed to be satisfied by traditional religions finding their validation through their longstanding participation in human culture. The Christian religion whose demise was predicted by many nineteenth century thinkers has outlived their memory. Only scholars now concern themselves with the likes of atheistic philosophers such as Schopenhauer, Stirner and Feuerbach. Nietzsche is a literary figure rather than a philosophical one. Christianity flourishes in the most developed areas of the world and in many undeveloped regions through the zeal of its missionaries. Islam which is hardly to be distinguished metaphysically from Christianity is having an explosive resurgence The forms of institutionalized metaphysics founded many centuries ago are alive and well throughout the planet existing side by side with the marvels of modern science.

It is not an original thought to wonder if the technological developments of the past two hundred years can be compared to the overblown armor that encased the dinosaurs of the Jurassic age. The age of dinosaurs came to an end because their bodies were too unwieldy and their brains too small to afford scope for evolutionary development. We do not know the exact details of the disappearance of dinosaurs but it is clear that there was no future for creatures weighted down by tons of armor and avoirdupois while possessing miniscule brains. The will-to-live of dinosaurs impelled them to an ever-enlarging body habitus that ultimately turned out to be self-defeating. There is a lesson to be learned here.

* * *

The fundamental necessity for a thinking person in the contemporary world is to establish a frame of reference within which he can place the enormous informational superstructure that has emerged during the era of technology. Like the narrator of Genesis, one must go back to the beginning to establish a clear sense of what has happened and how one distinguishes the *self* from the phenomenal world at large. This is not an easy task because the superstructure of society has become so vast and intimidating that only the boldest of individuals dare to attempt to transcend it. But the attempt must be made if one is to fulfill one's destiny as a member of the species *Homo sapiens*.

Will underlies all living existence. This is the basic metaphysical insight required for meaningful thought about life of any kind, including human life. The "will-to-live" is the iron rule out of which all other phenomena derive which have to do with living beings. Whoever concerns himself with life of any type must take this energy into account whether it be termed biological instinct, the *Wille* of Schopenhauer and Nietzsche, or a spirit within originating from a deity without.

Every age has its special tendencies that bedevil the people who live in it. Greco-Roman antiquity was obsessed by the ideal of "virtue" elaborated by antique philosophers; it was believed that character could be inculcated through education with little regard for human emotions or desires. The concept was logically coherent, the problem was that people at large were usually not content with virtue as a dominant ideal in and of itself. During the medieval era, "scholasticism" dominated the thought of the times. Elaboration of abstract ideas of God and His minions was believed to be a special path through which blessedness could be obtained. Scholastics of every type spun out complex ideas about the Divine Being and His relationship to human beings that gratified the doctors of the church and were foisted upon those with insufficient learning to question them.

Our era has discarded the antique Stoic notion of the Virtuous Citizen as well as the abstractions of medieval philosophers and theologians. We view Marcus Aurelius as a depressed personality and the Scholastics as precursors to the Inquisition and the Conquistadors. We have elaborated a radically new concept of fulfillment of the human condition based upon man as a creator of technology rather than an elaborator of thought. Human progress is thought to be a function of the scientific development which constantly strives to improve the comfort and power of the individual.

These tendencies are not due to changes in the capacities of human beings but rather to changing *values*. The Greco-Roman philosophers were familiar with technological innovation but had little interest in it. Medieval theologians put more value on belief than on behaviors. The leaders of modern technological society are fully capable of comprehending the views of the antique and medieval eras; however, they *value* their control over nature more than they do philosophical virtue or religious faith. The leaders of contemporary society derive enormous power from technology, a whole retinue of business executives, industrialists, scientists, lawyers and politicians obtain their prestige and affluence from the technology of modern science. The development of the interior self does not pay. Scientists, technicians and CEOs are the wisdom makers of our times, why should they interest themselves in worldviews that would only limit their importance?

Naturally, the trendsetters of a society represent only a tiny fraction of the population composing it. Underneath these leaders are the mass of people who rarely obtain to independent thought or behavior patterns. They admire to the point of worship what is held up to them as embodiments of progress whether it be antique philosophy, the metaphysics of the Christian era or the gadgets and contraptions of our technological times. When one views the history of humanity from afar, the pessimism of Schopenhauer becomes understandable, if not desirable as a personality trait.

The saving feature of humanity is its unique form of a will-to-live wiser than the temporal trends appearing in its history. When the superior individual is confronted with obstructions to his growth and development, i.e. to his will-to-live, means are found to overcome these obstructions. Human thought, which sometimes seems to be the greatest enemy of humanity, turns out to be its only savior. "Beware when the great God lets loose a thinker on this planet." The teaching, writing and personal example of independently thinking individuals are the means by which humanity finds new directions in its development. At least so it has been up to the present time.

* * *

"Every glance at the world . . . confirms and establishes that the *will-to-live*, far from being an arbitrary hypostasis or an empty expression, is the only true description of the world's innermost nature . . . it is the most real thing we know, in fact the kernel of reality itself." The monumental writings of Schopenhauer were to define this *will* and distinguish it from the bewildering array of derivative phenomena by which it manifests itself. Until one grasps the distinction between underlying*will* and its varied manifestations as perceived by the observer, philosophical knowledge does not exist. Instrumental research does not elucidate this will, it only describes the phenomena by which the will makes itself known. All the manifestations of life, all the genetic copying, all the mechanics of physiology which provide for the survival of the organism, all the procreative drives that result in its multiplication, all these are powered by the *will-to-live* and without which would all immediately cease their functioning.

Individuals perceive the will-to-live in living beings not as a unitary entity (which may be its essential nature) but as broken up into *organisms*. Through the variety and multiplicity of living organisms, there is an enormous range of possibilities for the expression of the will-to-live. Every individual organism is limited in space and time but behind these phenomenal constraints, all life is related in terms of sharing the will-to-live. There is great opportunity for metaphysical speculation here which I shall postpone for another time.

Schopenhauer believed the will-to-live was derived from more fundamental forces underlying all of nature. Along with the forces of gravity and electrochemical cohesion, there is now being recognized forces of repulsion driving planetary bodies apart. The will-to-live must be related to these fundamental forces of the universe in the way that erotic love is to sexual desire. An intuition of this concept was voiced by Empedocles at the dawn of Greek philosophy.

However one comprehends the will-to-live and its relation to the inanimate forces of the universe, it is a fatal error to fall into the trap of materialist thinking, i.e. that all manifestations of being are mechanical in nature and obey the law of causality. Such a vision of the universe misses the meaning of existence and is blind to the metaphysical need of human beings. Here is where Freud lost the thread of Schopenhauer who was more philosophically minded. Freud could not escape the influence of his neurological deterministic background. This is now the mentality of modern science dominating the thought of our times. In its depths, the materialist worldview comes from a denial of the destiny of *Homo sapiens* which is not to direct but to understand the universe.

If the will-to-live is the driving force behind all being, the unique feature of the human will-to-live is that it is conscious of itself and exhibits thought as its dominant manifestation. Without thought, there would be nothing special about human beings. Schopenhauer, who brilliantly worked out the concept of the will-to-live, did not seem to think that it was important that its manifestations in humans were unique. He inexplicably separated philosophical thought and artistic expression from the will-to-live. The natural outcome of such a separation is the pessimism with which Schopenhauer is associated.

Certainly all life has in common the effort to sustain itself and to procreate. But the various forms of life have their own unique characteristics; plants root themselves to grow while animals travel— through the air, in the sea on the land. Instinctual drives in animals, which is the term biology uses for the will-to-live, vary greatly. We humans have superimposed on the drives to survive and copulate, the drive to think, to understand, to reflect upon our surroundings. For this reason, man has been called a metaphysical animal or *Homo sapiens*.

* * *

We live in a mechanical era where virtually all the efforts of society are directed toward analysis and control of the phenomenal world of nature. There is much to be said for analysis and control of nature since it provides the basis for the leisure without which no non-utilitarian thought is possible. Most animals spend all their waking hours searching for food unless they are domesticated in which case they become bored and restless or lethargic and sleepy. Only humans are capable of utilizing leisure for metaphysical thought. The great error of our society is to imagine that technology can replace metaphysics. No amount of scientific investigation, no amount of genetic analysis or study of chemistry of the brain has been able to or will ever be able to explain the metaphysical nature of the will-to-live in human beings (or any other form of the will-to-live). Science can describe the copying of DNA or the transmission of impulses at synapses but this kind of analytic description does not explain the will-to-live. For this, the human soul is needed with its unique conceptual abilities. Human beings are mystical entities, one can describe their phenomenal qualities but no understanding of human nature is forthcoming from such descriptions. For this, a spiritual orientation is necessary which derives from the feeling, reflecting mind.

* * *

It is self-evident that there is no philosophy without a thinker who creates it just as there are no objects without the envisioning subject. These simple truisms are easily forgotten amidst the great sweeps of thought recorded by original thinkers, religious and secular, throughout history. There is no absolute truth just as there are no absolutely insightful individuals who record their ideas. All philosophic thought is a product of the times, the experience and the temperament of the thinker who produces it. Man may not be the measure of all things but he is certainly the measure of all his beliefs and ideas. The great minds of the past revealed what the human mind was capable of but they could not provide absolute truth. Every era has the obligation to go beyond them and mirror the new experiences and new conditions of new generations.

The new reality of the last two centuries is the revolution in scientific knowledge and technology which has absorbed virtually all the interest and energy of mentally gifted people. There is no aspect of human affairs at present which is not dominated by technology–housing, health, education, transportation, nutrition, politics, war–the list is endless. Even philosophy that only recently emancipated itself from theology is now close to becoming a branch of mathematics or possibly neurophysiology. The human will-to-live which from the perspective of Aristotle had evolved into the will-to-knowledge, now appears to have become the will-to-technology. *Homo sapiens* is becoming *Homo faber*, man the machine-maker. What was a relatively minor and often disparaged aspect of human affairs is now the dominant manifestation of the species. However, the more humans transform the world, the more their own inner being, the metaphysical will to develop and express themselves is moving off stage and becoming a lesser aspect of the human condition. Is this progress or retrogression?

Diogenes, the great Cynic of antiquity (not to be confused with the modern meaning of the word), once remarked that a philosophy which does not cure some ill of mankind had little worth. The Greek Cynics felt that their philosophy cured them of dependence on the artificial needs created by their society. Posterity and even many of their times felt that they took too extreme a view regarding freeing themselves of dependence on external things. But if there was ever an era which was in need of the Cynic idea, it is the modern world at the close of the second millennium. What good is our technological idolatry if it is associated with the loss of independence, trivialization of the mind and infantilization of taste. The destiny of man lies in the development of his spirit, mind, *Geist, Esprit*. Technology is detouring us in a direction from which there may be no return.

* * *

The journey from birth to death can be conceived of as a journey from will to soul. The newborn infant emerges from the womb as pure *will*, shrieking, struggling, gasping—a condition of animal willing unmodified by any superimposed mental direction. In time, he will learn about the nature of his environment through his contact with it. He learns to see, hear, speak, ambulate and understand. All this comes about through his contact with his external world. Right from the beginning, the dichotomy of self and the world, subject and object, determines the content of life from which humans are no exception. Even the deceptively simple phenomenon of sight is not merely a matter of visual stimulation but requires the construction of an image from the play of impulses upon the retina. The emergence of alimentary, motor and procreative activities occur in all animals in different forms according to their genetic endowment. It is humans alone, however, who develop the capacity for conscious, reflective thought composed of feelings, intuitions and concepts. I call this manifold of mental activities the *soul*.

The idea of a soul does not necessarily involve religious or eschatological doctrines that may be associated with this term. Additionally, it explains nothing to say that the soul is a resultant of neural activity in the brain. At the most, one can say that the human qualities defined by the term "soul" are associated with activity of cells composing the brain. One might equally say correctly that the soul is associated with breathing, beating of the heart or formation of urine by the kidney. None of these associations give much insight into the nature of human mental activities defined by the term soul. The most that can be said is that without normal bodily functions, including brain functions, the soul cannot develop or survive in human form.

An adequately functioning body is needed for the soul to emerge from raw primal will. But it is not enough to have a functioning body; stimuli from the outer world must occur to guide the infantile will into the adult soul. Stimuli are also not sufficient of themselves to produce this transformation but they are a necessary component of the process. A child locked up in a room throughout his life will become a pathetic degenerate instead of evolving a real soul. Without access to an outer world, the soul cannot form itself.

Initially, this access is through experience of physical world via the five senses. Nature is the great teacher of the child and children are inescapably drawn to her as soon as they capable of moving beyond the confines of their infant environment. Games of all kinds magnify the lessons of simple natural experiences. However, in time, all physical experiences give way to the one uniquely human form of experience–the experience of the human personality and the thoughts that it produces. Thoreau stated that real history is the history of great thoughts, all else is merely the whistling of the wind in the trees. It is exposure to great minds–in the broadest sense of the word–which more than any other form of experience helps form the soul.

* * *

Societies have learned that the application of technology to the physical environment we live in frequently has unforeseen consequences. Enlightened communities require studies of the environmental consequences of a project to determine how the project will affect the area in which it is located. Sometimes the consequences of the project may be so noxious to the environment that the project is not permitted to go forth. Societies that allow technology to run rampant without concern for unwanted consequences run serious risks of damaging their whole way of life. Witness the technological horror stories of the Stalinist Soviet Empire or the miserably ugly border areas of Mexico adjacent to the United States.

However, little attention is paid to the consequences of technologizing of daily life upon the human inner self, the soul. For every mechanization of human life, a price is paid through the diminished vitality of the soul. What is gained in the saving of physical energy is lost through diminishment of the soul in favor of the material aspect of existence. Where are the "great-soulled" persons of the twentieth century that might have been expected to appear in the western world by virtue of the "improvement" of life through labor-saving devices, mechanization of food production and conquering of disease. People live longer but their souls decay. Where are the Voltaires, Goethes, Emersons and Schopenhauers of the twentieth century, individuals whose own spiritual powers surpassed the limitations of their societies? They no longer exist or, if they do, they are not noticed by their societies. Our heroes are the scientists, politicians and professional entertainers who function in the world of things not ideas. Things are in the saddle and ride mankind as Emerson already noted by the middle of the nineteenth century in America. What would he have said of our current civilization? However, if he were alive today, no one would know what he said for no notice would be taken of him. Spirituality seems to be possible only when riding on the coattails of dogmatic religion or as part of a program of pleasuring the emotions. It appears that it is only the spokespersons of institutionalized Christianity (or the other main monotheisms) who have the capacity for principled resistance to the technological mentality of our era. The Pope in Rome today has more spiritual insight and power than independent individuals who rely on technology for heightened knowledge. Yet the Pope is a superannuated person leading a superannuated institution. It is tragic to see the enlightened western world relying on such a figure for spiritual inspiration.

Descartes is regarded as the father of modern western philosophy even though many of his ideas have not stood the test of time. His great contribution was to value the human mind as the distinctive feature of human beings. *Cogito ergo sum*–I think therefore I am– has sunken into the consciousness of western man. It is thinking in the broadest sense–reflecting, intuiting, willing, speaking, writing–which characterizes *Homo sapiens*. Subjectivity, i.e. the reflective self in thought, is what defines humans. Without subjectivity, we would be simply mechanical robots, totally determined by the physical aspects of our body and the instincts which subserve raw living. We are *human* to the extent that we are subjective. Kierkegaard claimed that the highest task for a human being is to become subjective. Kierkegaard's eccentricity caused him to adhere to the concept of Christianity but on the issue of subjectivity, he is the most inspired thinker in the annals of philosophy.

Subjectivity means to weigh the world according to our own values. Subjectivity is the opposite of objectivity, thus the latter ascertains truth through the objective methods of scientific study. Subjectivity is not suitable for science since science is predicated upon objective study of the universe. It is natural, therefore, to expect that a lifelong devotion to objectivity of thought will affect the subjective self and inhibit its development. If the body can be damaged by excessive labor in noxious mines, sweat shops or agricultural fields, why should not the soul be damaged by exclusive preoccupation with the objective minutiae of scientific endeavor. It is unreasonable to expect that one can forever inhibit the subjective self without some damage to the soul. Here is a subject worthy of the efforts of scientific psychology. Perhaps we shall find that an Emerson rather than an Edison or an Einstein should be the paragon of personal development held up to the youth of our society.

* * *

The human soul exhibits a will-to-know that has mysteriously evolved out of the will-to-live. What is the nature of the will-to-knowledge? Human behavior reveals it at all levels of development. The infant toddler searching out his environment reveals its first manifestations. Later, the interest in toys, games, animals and other humans enlarges the sphere of the will-to-know. Later still, the adolescent explores the world of his peers and begins to become aware of the worlds of art and higher learning. At the same time, the demands of family and society impinge upon the will-to-know, often ultimately reducing it to a poor remnant of its former self.

But it rarely disappears entirely, reminding its possessor that there is a metaphysical element to human life which transcends utilitarian needs. Some believe that the ultimate knowledge toward which all people strive is the knowledge of "God." But this word is not informative, referring more to human metaphysical need than to a knowable reality in the cosmos. One thing is certain, experience of the thoughts of great-soulled individuals is one of the principal manifestations of the will-to-know.

This will-to-know has been greatly corrupted by the utilitarian direction of contemporary technology. The unnatural preoccupation with what something is good for rather than what it is in itself is the dominant feature of the technological society. When the search for knowledge is justified by claims of utilitarian purpose, the metaphysical will-to-know is corrupted. Today, the desire for utilitarian "knowledge" has become a mania. One may ask to what end all this information? The one legitimate end of human effort is the development of the human soul. What does not contribute to this end is of no real value.

* * *

Reverence for one's own soul is an idea that requires careful and sustained thought. Schweitzer enunciated the doctrine of reverence for life but this is a notion which does not focus on the key issue, one's responsibility toward his own inner self. Life in general can be respected but the only entity worthy of a reverence that is not idolatry is the soul of the one who reveres. No one truly knows another living being so that the feeling of reverence cannot be translated into meaningful action. It is a travesty of nature to revere another life while neglecting one's own soul. In Fernando Pessoa's unique commentary on human life entitled *Book of Discontent* (September 19, 1931) exists the insight that acts of kindness are caprices which may have harmful consequences Too much harm has been done through reverence of other beings, whether they be living or dead There is an infinite difference between respecting other life and revering one's own inner self.

The absence of reverence for one's own soul has been encouraged by the teachings of Christianity that emphasizes an orientation toward others and a concept of the self as sinful. The person who has not developed a real reverence for his own soul is subject to all forms of decadence of self. In our time, this is principally manifested through idolatry of technology. The person whose interests and values are oriented to the material world of technology cannot attend to his own needs as a soul. It is a form of decadence to make a Faustian bargain with the world of technology that dispenses with development of the inner self.

The subjective self is the indispensable groundwork for the human condition. If this is ignored or treated as a mere accessory to the world of objects, then this groundwork begins to soften and turn into a morass on which no reliable footing is possible. Kierkegaard's clarion call in his *Concluding Unscientific Postscript* was that human truth is based upon human subjectivity. In last analysis, our own feelings about the world are what make us what we are. However, our age has been persuaded by the mandarins of science that the subjective self is a chimera, does not exist, is merely the epiphenomena of electrical signals emerging from a gray, pulpy, three pound lump sitting in the cranial cavity. If the self is an illusion, then what purpose is served by concentrating on its development? Better to concentrate on society and adaptation to it, on accumulating wealth, goods and power or the knowledge making such accumulations possible. Consequent to the enormous explosion of material development is the loss of consciousness of soul and the lack of interest in the processes that promote its growth. The Gospel admonition that it is of little use to acquire the whole world if one's soul is lost has been ignored in the pell-mell rush to jump on the technological band-wagon.

* * *

Outside me, the object world stands in bright clarity. Everything is objectified, all is clear, measurable, *quantitated*. Nature has been subjugated, the elements are controlled, at the flick of a switch, all the information known to man can be displayed in bright clarity on my screen. Not just things but behavior and relationships, *feelings*, are quantitated and brought under control. If one deviates from the prescribed norms, an army of regulation-wielding functionaries swings in action to control the offending individual. The avenues of the most sacred personal expression–sex, work, relationships–have been brought under societal control, regulated, quantitated, objectivized according to the prescribed social norms. There is a System, created by politicians, regulated by lawyers, powered by wealth, which controls life in all its facets and directs it into predetermined channels. Unbelievable arrogance of power! What will become of human life?

But still underneath this enormous System, there pulsates the human will that has created it all. The System is like a great, glittering palace with fantastic mechanisms for ensuring gratification of bodily needs for all and unparalleled wealth for a few. The humans in the palace have long since forgotten–if they ever knew at all–the origin of the mechanisms which satisfies their needs. Yet it is a man-made system energized by a mysterious source of power. Should this power ever fail, the great palace would collapse into a chaotic heap for want of the energy to sustain it.

So it is with the System of western society which is sustained by the force of human faith in it. The faith is that the individual is served by the mechanistic devices which powers its progress. But what if this faith should be shaken? What if the interior being called the soul loses faith in the mechanistic world it has created? What if all the stuff, all the securities, all the contraptions which today seem to be the substance of the good life are not good for the soul? The masses rush toward mechanization of existence, things are in the saddle and still ride mankind. But will it always be so? Can the human will be always so subjugated to man-made mechanisms?

I have digressed. The thesis is the transformation of raw will into soul. More to the point, perhaps, is what kind of soul shall emerge from this transformation. Nietzsche conceived the idea of the Will to Power that he saw as the necessary corrective to hypocritical Christian morality dominating European society. It is interesting that Nietzsche was never able to organize his idea into a coherent whole, it was left to the executors of his literary estate to lay the philosophical foundation for German National Socialism. I believe Nietzsche's premature collapse was due in part to his recognition of the bankruptcy of his great idea. Whatever Nietzsche was, he was an honest and clairvoyant thinker who would give up untenable ideas.

The conventional Judeo-Christian wisdom is that the raw will-to-live becomes transformed–through divine intervention–into a will to morality. What we live today is an amalgam of the will-to-power and the will-to-morality. What is missing is the will-to-know. Not "know" as information but "know" as apprehension of a deeper reality.

* * *

The honest writer needs not only to express himself according to his tastes and temperament but also needs to give an account of his motives. Writing is difficult and requires effort, one should be clear about its purpose. Why does one write? More specifically and more relevantly, why do I write? I do not gain a living for myself, I do not acquire reputation; there is more likelihood that I will win the California lottery than that either of the aforesaid events will occur. Nor do I painlessly kill time as I might were I on a golf course or in my garden. No, I write because I have the irresistible intuition that by writing I develop my inner self. This is an idea I have expounded before and will expound again. I write to form my soul by bringing into conscious being the vague unformed feelings which moil and toil inside of me. I create my reality...

* * *

A little late evening metaphysics. Schopenhauer asserted that the "intellect" is the epiphenomenon of the brain–as have many neuroscientists of the present time. However, this idea is a contradiction of Schopenhauer's whole philosophy as pointed out by his later critics. That intellect is something separate from will is mere obscurantism. The awareness of self upon which all real philosophy is based does not distinguish between will and intellect, both are aspects of the self and cannot be separated from one another. The conscious self and unconscious self form a unity even if their manifestations may have different forms. Schopenhauer's great conception of the world to be either "will" or representation by "will" requires that the brain be viewed as the representation of the intellect just as the total body is the representation of the unified will. Brain and body are the *phenomenal* forms of the individual. Just as there can be no representation of will except as a physical body so the representation of intellect takes form as a space-occupying brain. But representing something is very different from knowing it.

The metaphysical need which exists in humans is often satisfied by belief in traditional religions clothed in piety, worship, faith, etc. A better way, however, to satisfy one's metaphysical need is through intellectual expansion of the soul so as to move beyond the naive materialism of the untutored mind. The intellectualized soul provides the means of apprehending the human position within the cosmos–an assertion made by Heraclitus at the dawn of western philosophy. Thus consciousness of self leads to consciousness of all, the key thought underlying Hindu cosmology. The only external beings worthy of a degree of reverence are those great individuals who have enlarged the scope of human consciousness. A connection with these great minds is the one form of communication which is really worthwhile. The will-to-know is the metaphysical need of *Homo sapiens* forcefully asserting itself.

The soul may be defined as the primordial will-to-live of humans transfigured into the will-to-know. Reverence for one's own soul means reverence for the striving to know the nature of being. When one is secure in the reverence of one's own will-to-know, the reductionism of scientists and mythologies of priests with respect to this striving become ridiculous and unworthy of serious thought about the soul.

Schopenhauer's fundamental insight was to realize that while knowledge of the phenomenal world was obtained through the senses and their instrumental extensions, knowledge of the basic force driving all phenomena could only be acquired by analogy through self awareness. He "searched himself out" as few have done since Heraclitus and found the universal will pervading existence. His pessimism, obsession with science and peculiar belief in the separation of will and intellect are extraneous ideas, more related to his temperament than to his fundamental insight. The concept of will-to-live provides the necessary groundwork for the understanding of being. Will, as Schopenhauer conceived it, is the energy underlying all phenomena, the "thing-in-itself" which manifests its energies through appearance of the world of phenomena. Modern physics has fully confirmed Schopenhauer's insight.

Others who have searched themselves have described what they found somewhat differently. Kierkegaard found God, Max Stirner found "Der Einzige" needing to live itself out. Nietzsche tried to settle on the Will to Power but it contradicted his basic values. Feuerbach found humanity, Berdyaev creativity, and Heidegger *Angst*. Generations of Christian mystics have found Jesus Christ. One may wonder whether there is such a thing as metaphysical "truth." Or is truly "man the measure of all things" and skepticism the only means of preserving an intellectual conscience?

Not being a scholar, I will leave to professors and priests the task of reconciling the views of the great minds who have had their moment on the stage of culture. I should like to have my say on this stage, especially since my era seems to be one singularly devoid of metaphysical minds who have something to offer on the subject. Searching out my own self, I discover a force dominating my life as long as I can remember. I have always had the desire to know new things: explore new territories foreign to me, learn new languages, meet people from different cultures, apprehend new ideas, acquire new skills, experience the shock of erotic encounter. Slowly, very slowly, I acquired the confidence to generate and explore my own thoughts. This will to "know"–I use this word in its broadest sense– is a bright thread that runs through an otherwise mundane life. I have come to appreciate the thought with which Aristotle begins his *Metaphysics*: "All men by nature desire to know."

The will-to-live within me, with many missteps and painful contradictions, has been slowly transformed into a will-to-know that, in my opinion, is the proper state for *Homo sapiens*. This writing itself is my effort to *clarify* my thoughts on the real questions in my life. My faith is that through my will-to-know, I can create my soul and that no other activity approaches this one in importance. Assertions about knowledge of God will is to me a presumption, if not a blasphemy; the only spiritual experience I can attest to is that of knowing my own will. Like De Vigny in his *Journal*, I say that since God has not spoken to me, I have nothing to say about him. *Rends-lui silence pour silence.* Contact with the great metaphysical minds of the past is my form of worship and facilitates my personal development. What is least acceptable of all to me is the shallow attitude that mere knowledge of phenomena– objective science–is sufficient for fulfillment of my will-to-know. That path is leading my society toward insect existence. It is better to endure the uncertainties of metaphysical knowledge than in live in the spiritual desert of technologically oriented science.

* * *

Where are the Kierkegaards, Schopenhauers, Nietzsches and Berdyaevs of the postwar twentieth century? They do not exist as cultural figures. If they did, they would have no more possibility of reaching the public at large than do wolves have for survival in a modern city. The costly phenomena-based technology of today has rendered literary expression of the soul all but impossible. What Emerson said an eternity ago:

"Things are in the saddle and ride mankind"

has become the absolute rule of modern life. The distinction between man and machine is disappearing. No one really believes any longer in that *ding-an-sich* called the soul, spirit, the inner self, the *élan vitale* or however one wishes to express the apprehension that human life–*all life*–consists of something which transcends nucleic acids, proteins and membranes. The naive view of reality has taken hold of the mind, largely due to the magic-like power of technology. However the smooth surfaces of modern civilization may prove to be volcanic underneath, as Nicolai Berdyaev used to claim. Either we will ultimately revert to insect life, abandoning the inner dynamism of spirit, or volcanic eruptions are in the offing. In my view, the latter is more likely since spirit cannot be extinguished by technological means.

Phenomena-based technology that fundamentally serves the will-to-live must give way to the thoughts that serve the will-to-know. Technology has its subordinate value in human life but this value has become enormously overblown to the detriment of the will-to-know. Like some financial bubble that expands through its own inertia, technological development goes on and on and on. Humanity everywhere has become converted to the idea that technological progress and human progress are one and the same thing. It is faith in this idea that powers technology; should this faith be lost, a societal revolution will occur greater than any collapse of empires or belief systems of the past. This revolution must occur since there is no truth in the idea that technological progress is equivalent to human progress. It cannot be true because the mechanisms and consequences of technology are unrelated to the real wellspring of the human condition, the human soul.

The rapid progress of technology in Euro-American societies may be due, at least in part, to the inability of institutionalized Christianity provide an effective counterweight to the achievements of modern science. The dogmas of Christian belief have long since lost their power to provide a conceptual basis for real spirituality. The Christian god is dead, as Nietzsche proclaimed, it has become a mere totem or idol, no different than the totems or ideals of primitive tribes. Christian philosophers like Kierkegaard or Teilhard de Chardin succeed in developing their own thoughts by bitterly criticizing or virtually ignoring the churches and dogmas of their day. Were there a viable spiritual culture in the western world today, the massive erosion of spiritual life by technology would not have occurred. Such a culture is sorely needed.

* * *

As an old neurologist, let me express some thoughts about the brain. This undistinguished three pound lump of protoplasm is said to be the originator of that most remarkable creation of nature, the human mind. How could this absurdity, this idea violating all common sense and against what the deepest minds of humanity have thought throughout recorded history have come to receive general acceptance? This inauspicious chunk of tissue has been dissected, analyzed, magnified, and subjected to the most elaborate electrical and chemical studies with the hope of understanding the human mind. All to no avail, the mind and the brain are as far apart today as in the time of Descartes. Nothing has been forthcoming of interest to a philosopher except that creatures possessed of a brain cannot function when it is damaged and die if the damage is extensive. Yet the search goes on and on; instead of scientists becoming more philosophically minded, philosophers are becoming more like scientists. There has now appeared the phenomenon of "neurophilosophers." As William James once remarked, our professors of philosophy would wear white coats if they dared.

What is the explanation of this unfounded credulity by the most educated strata of society? I say it is the failure to grasp the distinction between the phenomenal and noumenal worlds so clearly stated by Kant, clarified by Schopenhauer and amply confirmed by the failure of subatomic physics to discover a particulate universe. The phenomenal world of the senses–no matter how magnified by modern instrumentation–is not a true picture of what exists. The scientist can systematize phenomena and control their causal relationships but never, never through scientific observations can the nature of the forces underlying material existence be *comprehended*. This is as true for the force of gravity as it is for the nature of the mind. Science has grown so used to controlling phenomena that it no longer believes in the existence of any other aspect of reality. But every human being possessed of a modicum of wisdom knows that his own conscious being expresses a world not accessible to technological study. And what exists in each individual self exists more or less in all other living selves. It is only the naively childish beliefs of contemporary science which has permitted the obsession with technology to flourish.

* * *

Schopenhauer again. The fundamental *einziger Gedanke* of Schopenhauer, his 'single thought,' was the concept of *will* as the underlying reality of all existence. He might have used terms like force or energy or drive equally to refer to his concept of a nonmaterial power underlying the apparent solidity of the phenomenal world. He deserves a honored place in the annals of philosophy for his expostulation of this idea which advances beyond the naïve realism of every day life. However, having said that he had a single thought to communicate, Schopenhauer went on to elaborate this thought in the most arrogant style imaginable. He committed the cardinal sin of making negative value judgments on the realities behind the phenomenal world. The individual will is without meaning and only a source of endless suffering. Salvation is to be found only in renunciation of the will-to-live. Death is the great opportunity to no longer be I. And so on and so forth until Schopenhauer virtually crosses the threshold into the Christian mentality of otherworldliness. *Nirvana* belief is adopted *in toto* without reservation. One easily tires of Schopenhauer and grows annoyed with his schoolmaster-like manner of writing. Hypocrisy is the obvious accusation to level against him since he was a bon vivant in his daily life and craved the recognition of society. Nietzsche who started out as his admiring disciple finally grew to hate his influence.

Nevertheless, one cannot throw out the baby with the bath water. Schopenhauer was a great thinker who has much to say to our times. There is no penetrating into reality without understanding the Schopenhaurian doctrine of the world as will and representation. The English-reading world is fortunate to have the E.F.J. Payne translation of his monumental work. It is a sad irony to think that today Schopenhauer is known as the great pessimist instead of the author of the concept of the universality of will. In our era, when materialism dominates all facets of life and few individuals have the slightest interest in grasping the reality behind appearances, Schopenhauer's insight is needed more than ever. But it needs to be purged of its devaluation of the individual will.

The place where Schopenhauer begins to go seriously astray is in his concepts of knowledge and consciousness. It is worth noting that contemporary biologists have taken up Schopenhauer's idea that consciousness is merely an adaptation of the organism for facilitating survival (in S.'s terminology–the will to live). He is rarely given credit for his ability to foresee modern biological thought. In any case, Schopenhauer passionately defends his thesis that conscious knowledge is merely the servant of the will to live. Only when knowledge is disconnected from the will does it become the agent of liberation from life drives. Thus Schopenhauer may be placed in the camp of those who view consciousness as an "epiphenomenon" of brain processes.

This view greatly weakens the integrity of Schopenhauer's philosophical position that there is a "metaphysical being" underlying the phenomenal world. How can the mind be a "phenomenon" of the brain when the brain itself is the phenomenon of the will? Why should consciousness be relegated to phenomenal status when it appears so clearly to be an elaboration of will? This contradiction was noted by professional philosophers like Windelband and used to undermine his position. Schopenhauer's rejection of mind and consciousness as primary being, the *Ding-an-Sich*, naturally leads to quietism, pessimism and a Buddhist philosophy of life. Although Schopenhauer was not a naive realist, it is easy to lump together will, mind and consciousness and view all mental life as an epiphenomenon of brain functions.

Schopenhauer's genius lay in his intuition of the nature of the relationship between will and phenomena. He advanced beyond Kant in recognizing that the inner aspect of all things consisted of an energy which he called "will." The will of a piece of rock manifests itself through the forces of cohesion, inertia and gravity. These are different only in degree from the will to live of living beings reacting to stimuli and the will to know of humans responding to inner motives and generating abstract thought. The will of a developed human being is radically different from the will of a plant or a cow. It manifests itself not merely in the will-to-live but also in the will-to-know.

* * *

Homo sapiens is a creature who strives to *know*. The pattern is evident—every living human began life as a raw unformed "will," gradually evolving during its development into a personality which seeks out experience and knowledge. The search begins modestly during infancy expressing itself as a desire to explore its environment and familiarize itself with the objects in it. Piaget described this process in great detail initiating the scholarly study of child mental development. With time, the child's goals expand; the adolescent wants to learn about the wider world beyond his immediate environment, especially to experience the*relationships* that are the greatest of all learning experiences. Travel, other languages, art, science and philosophy ultimately are the means by which the "will to knowledge" expresses itself unless the hard vicissitudes of life interfere with the fulfillment of these desires. The older person, once relieved of the burdens of career and family, may continue to exhibit this will to know which characterizes *Homo sapiens.*

All living things strive actively to become what is possible for them. There is a destiny for every living creature which it struggles to reach during its life. The human destiny is the acquisition of knowledge in its broadest sense, in spite of the frailty of the human organism. "A thinking reed" is how Pascal designated the human condition. This knowledge—wisdom is perhaps the better word—is not confined to information about the phenomenal world. Science is not enough to satisfy the human will to know. Within himself, every human being can recognize—if he cares to look closely—a metaphysical will which transcends the material universe. He desires to know the nature of this will and its relationship to the universe of being. Any worldview that ignores or denies the metaphysical reality within him cannot ultimately satisfy his will to know.

The techniques of managing life in a world of *materia* are tools, not ends in themselves. The great delusion of our times is the unstated habit of mind that the means of technique can supplant the ends of knowledge. The most important activity of human beings is the acquisition of the knowledge that is an end in itself—which is why the loss of leisure, the necessary background for reflective living, is such a serious problem in contemporary society.

The term "wisdom" designates the hoped-for state to which knowledge brings human beings. It is a virtual condition since the life we know has never brought men to the state of completed wisdom. Antique society could never find the "wise man" toward which the ancient schools of philosophy aspired. Great religions like Brahmanism and Christianity have provided theoretical frameworks for wisdom but no institution founded on a body of dogmas can substitute for the individual who strives to know the world through knowing himself.

* * *

Schopenhauer shrank back from the task of discovering the meaning of the human condition. By disconnecting knowledge from the human will, he stamped his thought with a pessimism that vitiated much of its value for others. It also provided an intellectual basis for Freudian psychoanalysis which absolutely rejects any metaphysical aspect of the human will.

What does not enlighten me diminishes me. The heritage of Schopenhauerism *in toto*, and its offspring Freudianism, has been a diminution of the human condition. Schopenhauer and Freud were inheritors of the European tradition of respect for the individual mind, however one defines this entity. This capital of this tradition is almost exhausted now as a consequence of the relentless scientific materialism that has expanded into every aspect of culture. The limitless depth of the human psyche once proclaimed by Heraclitus has been replaced by the dictum of neuroscience that mind and consciousness are illusory epiphenomena of neural networks. Not the wise man but the computer is the central feature of education. No doubt there is a practical aspect to this preference; computers are everywhere but individuals with even a particle of wisdom are hard to find. But the truth will out some day. If a culture is founded upon a way of life which involves a misconception of the human condition and its destiny, it must ultimately give way to a different culture which is more attuned to the reality of *Homo sapiens*.

* * *

It is probably no accident that the scientific revolution first occurred in the christianized western world. Christians have tended to believe that the enormous industrial progress of the last few centuries have had something to do with the Christian faith. God must have blessed the Christian way of life. However, there is another explanation. Christianity may have become so weak as a religion, so lacking in metaphysical substance, that its dogmas and traditions were unable to prevent western man from breaking out into new forms of thought–scientific thought. There is little doubt that there are beneficial aspects to this new form of thought with respect to knowledge of phenomena, control of nature, and creation of technologies enhancing human potential. But now science is the dominant force in human life, it has displaced religion in most ways and has evolved the dogma that technological progress is identical to human progress. Not long ago, a president of General Motors, the largest automotive manufacturer in the United States (and the world) stated categorically that what was good for General Motors was good for the United States. This mentality exists today regarding technological development in general. But what if this not be true? What if every new device produced today by the engineers of technology results in a diminishment of the human mind through economic pressures, loss of leisure and progressive decay of the awareness of a metaphysical self? For those who have abandoned or never achieved the consciousness of a metaphysical self, such an idea is antiquated and reactionary. But nothing true is antiquated or reactionary Truth is the only thing worth dedicating one's life to acquire. The consciousness of a metaphysical self antedates modern science and is based upon an awareness that is independent of modern science. Much learning, according to the ancients, does not teach knowledge but becomes *kakotechnie*–evil artfulness.

* * *

The profoundest minds of the world have all concluded that there is a transcendental force (will, soul, spirit, mind) underlying reality. This was the view of the Brahmanic sages, Spinoza, Rousseau, Goethe, Emerson, Schopenhauer, Kierkegaard, Teilhard de Chardin–to name some well known figures in the history of thought. Determining the nature of the relationship of the individual to this force is the principal question facing a person who has regard for his real self. Evading this question through preoccupation with the minutiae of daily life is the cardinal error humans commit.

There are no prearranged answers to the transcendental question. What has been abundantly clear at all times is that the chatter of the world interferes with consideration of the question. A person without leisure, without respite from the constant noise and stimuli emanating from society, especially technological society, cannot hope to work out his relationship to the transcendental which I will now presume to call by its accustomed name–God. This word 'God' has been so misused in recorded history that one hesitates to even pronounce it much less to write it. But it is the word that commonly designates what is meant by a transcendental force and so it cannot be avoided. Every human being needs to work out his relationship with God. All other causes must give way to this essential task. No traditions, no dogmas, no holy book, no substitute of whatever nature can perform this task for him. If he does not sense that he has a soul in touch with the transcendental, that this soul is different in nature from what he perceives material substance to be, then he cannot develop this relationship. If his mind is committed to materialism as the only reality of his existence, he has sold out his spiritual endowment. If he avoids the question of the transcendental in his existence, he has abdicated his responsibility to himself as a thinking person, as *Homo sapiens*. Only through searching out his own self can he come to terms with his place in existence.

One can imagine that God finds no peace except in the developed minds of the entities that his will has created. This is a personal attitude of mine that has gradually come to me over the years. Others may develop profounder concepts of the relationship of humans to the transcendental force named God. I myself may arrive some day at a different formulation about my relationship to the transcendental (I still shrink from the G word.) Yet at this moment in time I am convinced that my will to know represents this relationship. God is not complete without my thought.

This writing is an extension of my will to know. All my writings are fundamentally a manifestation of my desires in this direction since putting thoughts on paper is the most powerful way I know to establish my ideas. In this sense, I conceive of my writing as "God's work."

"Ich weiss, dass ohne mich Gott nicht ein Nu kann leben
Werd ich zu nicht, er muss von Not den Geist aufgeben."

Angelus Silesius

* * *

The obsession with objects dominates my society. Freud stated that religion was the universal obsessive neurosis of humanity but I claim that objects deserve this label, especially money, which is the abstract representation of all objects of desire. The untransfigured will to live results in an overwhelming desire for possessing objects which fortify this will; without transformation of the will to live to a will to know, the obsession with material objects is inevitable. Humans must will something, if it is not to apprehend the transcendental, spiritual aspect of life then it will be to plunge into its material aspect.

The failure to fully grasp the dualistic nature of the human condition—as most effectively set forth by Schopenhauer—results in a one-sided monism that can be either spiritual or material in nature. The forest sages of Hindu tradition developed the view that spirit was all, the inner self was equated with "God" (Atman=Brahman) and that the object world was an illusion (Maya) not to be taken seriously. Buddhism essentially took over this point of view and refined it into a more coherent way of life. Hindu origin philosophies are monistic at their core; spirit is the only reality. Schopenhauer was attracted to this view although he lived his life according to a dualistic conception. Out of the Hindu-Buddhist worldview grows a resignation and disinterest toward the object world. Superimposed upon a personality oriented to movement and creativity, it easily leads to a deep pessimism toward all things.

Modern western culture has developed toward a diametrically opposite position from Hindu thought. Objects are the sole reality, the world of spirit is the illusion. The scientific object-oriented culture of the west has conferred great material power upon humanity but has left it spiritually bankrupt. The desire for a sense of self and for knowledge of the reality lying behind the object world is not satisfied by object experience and object possession. Freud's belief that only "scientific work" can lead to knowledge of reality, that it is an illusion to expect anything from intuition or introspection has turned out to be a fateful error for western society. Freud, who was a remarkable personality, has had an impact on western society that far transcends the confines of the psychoanalytic organizations. Freud did not accept, or perhaps did not know, Schopenhauer's conviction that a system of physics without metaphysics is untenable, that humans carry the ultimate secrets of being within themselves.

Nowhere is the problem of western science more evident than in the mind-brain controversies that have emerged ever since nineteenth century anatomists began a methodical study of the human brain. The simple direct inspection of brains has given way to the most esoteric investigational studies utilizing all the resources of modern neuroanatomy and neurophysiology. Although the issues have little changed, the discourse on the subject has deteriorated into learned technical discussions. There is no William James who was at once philosopher and psychologist who can shed light on the essential nature of the problem. For anyone who wishes to understand the real issue involved in the mind-brain problem, there is still no substitute for James' *Principles of Psychology*, first published in 1890. There he concludes, after the most exhaustive analyses, that " . . . nature in her unfathomable designs has mixed us of clay and flame, of brain and mind, that the two things hang indubitably together and determine each other's being, but how or why, no mortal may ever know." James did not think that humans

were "conscious automatons" as the exponents of the computer
theory of the brain would have us believe. It is worth noting that
James lost interest in scientific psychology after publication of his
monumental work, asserting that everything of real interest to him
lay outside the realm of scientific psychology. He never would
agree to return to it for a second edition.

* * *

What does the word "metaphysical" mean? It seems to have first
come into use by the compilers of Aristotle's unpublished writings
who used it to designate a group of treatises which were separate
from those dealing with "physics" (physics included biology and
psychology.) Aristotle himself is said to have designated these
treatises variously as First Philosophy, Theology or Wisdom. One
may say that they were concerned with the antique concept of
"Logos," the regulatory system of existence comprehending the
more specific modes of knowledge.

The use of the word "metaphysics" is almost as objectionable
today as the word "God." Consideration of the Logos of existence
requires experience, discipline of mind and a knowledge of human
recorded thought. It is not a subject for the ignorant or the self-
indulgent. We humans are the product of what has gone before us
and we ignore the history of thought to the detriment of our own
minds. A most serious problem today is the lack of integrity of
those who claim to be teachers of metaphysics. The essential element
of metaphysical thought is valuation of the spirit above *materia*.
When the goal of metaphysical teaching is the accumulation of
wealth for the teacher, then metaphysical teaching becomes corrupt
and is deprived of its integrity.

The expression of metaphysical thought, if it is not to be merely
a didactic compilation of the ideas of others, depends on the state
of mind of the one who is expressing himself. He must *value* his
thoughts above all else. Monetary recompense represents a value
diametrically opposed to the valuation of thought. It represents

the commitment to the object world. One may pay publishers or bookstores for access to the thoughts of Nietzsche but to pay Nietzsche himself would be unimaginable. Nietzsche wrote with his blood; one does not pay another for his metaphysical blood. Socrates recognized this problem when he distinguished sophists from philosophers like himself by the fact that the former took money for their activities. As a rule of thumb, one may say that the purveyor of a metaphysics *emanating from their own thought* cannot benefit financially without grave risks of corrupting themselves. There is no place for material motives in metaphysical thought, it is a contradiction in terms.

The metaphysical spirit is weak in the human condition. Humans must eat. Socrates accepted free dinners and tokens of appreciation from his circle of friends. Schopenhauer received royalties in his old age and Berdyaev lived in a house donated by his admirers. But these were lesser and secondary rewards. It is always clear where the primary motivation lies in the heart of those genuinely committed to the realm of metaphysical thought.

* * *

There is a metaphysical concept underlying technological society. It is that the proliferation of technique with the corresponding increase of available *materia* will be *fulfilling* to the human spirit. The entire free enterprise market system is founded upon this article of metaphysical faith. Certainly material progress has beneficial effects for many individuals at different times in their lives. The question is whether human individuals are well served by assimilating this faith *in toto*. There are examples of sects who have consciously rejected this faith–the Amish in the United States, for example–these are people with a living metaphysical belief that replaces the faith in material progress. Such examples are rare in western society; generally, there are no challengers to the metaphysics of material progress. Nominal belief in the traditional western religions cannot compete with the faith in technology.

If one closely examines the faith in material progress, it becomes evident that, like all faiths, it precludes belief in other metaphysical beliefs. Just as one cannot be a devout Christian and a devout Hindu simultaneously, so one cannot be a believer in the inevitable benefits of material progress while simultaneously believing in the reality of the human spirit. The two beliefs are not compatible. One can give superficial acknowledgement to one or the other but both cannot be enthroned on the altar of genuine faith at the same time. Either a human being envisions himself as a material entity with secondary "spiritual" qualities–epiphenomena in the language of philosophy–or as a spiritual being with material characteristics. One or the other will be preeminent in the human mind, the second choice must take a secondary place.

Our scientific culture has resulted in a way of life and a way of belief in which the material viewpoint is predominant. Everything about the modern western society toward which all the rest of the planet aspires promotes the materialist worldview. The idea of the human spirit has become an empty shell toward which only lip service is given. But truth will out in the long run. *Primo impendere vero*, to dedicate oneself to truth, was not only a guideline for Schopenhauer, it is an inborn tendency of *Homo sapiens*. Every human being wants to know the truth; by truth he means the truth of human intuition, not scientific truth. If he becomes convinced that the truth does not lie in the materialist world view, then the bubble of technological society will collapse like the tulip craze or the South Sea island mania of centuries past.

Serious thinkers from Plato to Schopenhauer, from Aristotle to Sir Arthur Eddington, have realized that the materialist worldview is based on the mastery of *materia*, not metaphysical truth. We are physical as well as spiritual beings; management of material facilitates our material life. But to the extent that vital energies are expended on physical being, to that extent they are withdrawn from spiritual being. To that extent we return to the animal life from which we arose. The will to live dominates the will to know. The person who devotes all his energies to *materia* becomes spiritually defunct. It makes no difference whether he is a slave laboring in a mine or on a field or is a nuclear physicist giving his principal mental energies to scientific work. Where one's treasure is, there will be found his heart's desire.

Western man seems to be on his way to becoming the conscious automaton decried by nineteenth century thinkers. One cannot devote himself to a world of *materia* without such a consequence unfolding. Could this be the ultimate destiny of our species, to become conscious automata symbiotic with computers and other machines? It is unlikely that our political leaders will resemble those of Samuel Butler's *Erewhon* where all new technological development was banned. Can the land of the Hyperboreans be the only refuge for those who reject the metaphysics of dominant technology?

Well, of course, I do not know. Yet I think that the desire for metaphysical truth is stronger than the habits of any particular society. I wish to believe that the destiny of humans to become spiritual beings with independent minds is stronger than western society's tendency toward producing conscious automatons. In last analysis, subjection to the world of technology is no different from subjection to the world of uncontrolled nature. Man labors blindly in the service of one or the other. But humans are irresistibly drawn to the life of the spirit however it may manifest itself and through this life to an understanding of the metaphysical being of which they are a part. Sooner or later, they are bound to emancipate themselves from any type of slavery that impedes their spiritual development.

* * *

Every thinking person during the course of his life develops a concept of existence determining the values he lives by. At different times, in different places, under different circumstances, these concepts change and alter one's life. Within different societies, concepts of existence differ. The ancient Greeks were attuned to glory early in the course of their development, then to wisdom. Homer was famous among the Greeks because he artistically conceptualized the life of glory; later his works ossified into a holy scripture much as the Judeo-Christian Bible has in western society. Later, philosophers replaced Homer as the new heroes of Greek culture.

The Christian era in the west inaugurated the discovery of spirituality. Jesus Christ became a force in the world because a small group of Messianic-oriented Jews accepted him as their Messiah. His unique spiritual message overcame the "pagan" traditions and carried Europe into an age where the concept of spirit became dominant. The whole philosophic movement of the antique world disappeared into obscurity with the exception of Plato and Aristotle whose works served certain purposes for the doctors of the Christian churches.

Today, the concept of spirit has largely waned and we live under the sign of scientific materialism. The unimaginable successes of technology in controlling nature has provided a powerful underpinning for this new concept, much as miracles reinforced the spiritual power of Jesus of Nazareth. The attitude toward things of the spirit is largely traditional, analogous to respect for one's buried ancestors; it represents allegiance to the past rather than orientation to the future. What stirs men's imagination for the future is the technology to be created by scientific materialism. The only living faith is the belief that monistic materialism–the concept that only *materia* exists–is the basis of all reality. Out of this belief grows the preoccupation with the possession and utilization of material things, the products of technology. Money, of course, as the abstract representation of all material things, becomes the overwhelming object of desire.

It is unlikely that the technological revolution that has given rise to the expectation of permanent technological "progress" can really deliver this progress to the five billion inhabitants of our planet. This might have been a possibility in the era of Descartes when the earth's population was a tenth of what it is now. More and more, the global population is being divided into haves and have nots, into an elite who enjoy the magic of technological progress and a far more numerous mass of have nots whom technology has condemned to an overcrowded, uncertain existence. This latter group may yearn for the fruits of technology but few of them will receive them. It is not possible to Europeanize the world. The survival of the species in peace is dependent upon valuation of spiritual development above material development. The philosophy of the Greek Cynics, of Thoreau and Emerson, of Nietzsche and Berdyaev is what will be needed in place of the dangerous illusions of the Circes of technology. The will to wisdom must replace the will to riches if we are to survive. The saying of Emerson that fulfillment is to be found in plain living and high thinking will have to become a reality instead of a cliché if real progress is occur in human society.

The old Christian spirituality is no longer a possibility. The new spirituality will not be principally an orientation toward religious tradition but will be an encompassing of the spiritual experiences that humanity has shown itself capable of undergoing. The enlightened individual will have reverence for only one thing— his own soul. He will seek out the experience and the learning that will develop his soul to the greatest possible extent. The cult of technique will be maintained only to the degree necessary to support the life of the spirit. Much of this support will be directed toward maintaining a healthy body but the fiction that a fulfilling life can be indefinitely prolonged will be abandoned and death will be permitted its proper place in the life of a spiritually developed person.

* * *

A necessary presupposition of any philosophical viewpoint is an understanding of the phenomenal nature that is the principal concern of most people. By an understanding of phenomenal nature, I mean awareness that all human experience passes through the prism of a complex sensorineural apparatus. The nature of the brain and its connected neural extensions are at least as important in determining our images of the outer world as are the objects which give rise to these images. This awareness was first brought into being by Immanuel Kant in his epoch-making treatise *Critique of Pure Reason* and remains valid to this day. Two centuries of brain research has enormously elaborated our knowledge of the structure of this organ (although not how it produces images) but has not altered the validity of Kant's insight about how we see the world.

Kant's concepts have passed into common knowledge even if few people are familiar with his contributions given the turgidity of most German philosophical prose. The discoveries of particle physics regarding the nature of matter have greatly supported Kantian theory. That simple brown flat table we perceive is really an unbelievably complex mass of whirling "particles" which are really electrical forces. The simple color, shape and density of the table are illusions foisted upon us by the limitations of our perceptual apparatus. These illusions are necessary because the human imaging ability could not possibly cope with the complex maelstrom constituting ,simple material objects. Simplicity of matter is an illusion created by the brain.

If what Kant referred to as "transcendental esthetics" is now a scientific commonplace, not so is a related concept advanced with similar power a generation later by Arthur Schopenhauer. *The World as Will and Representation* was published in three editions over a forty year period (1819—1859) during Schopenhauer's lifetime. In this monumental work, Schopenhauer worked out his concept that the reality behind phenomenal experience is "Will" which he conceived of as the *metaphysical* force underlying the world of phenomena. Schopenhauer's ideas have had little influence on modern thought, especially thought in the English-speaking world. Schopenhauerism was once important among European intellectuals; one might wonder if a perverted version of it appears in the film *The Triumph Of Will* which was made to commemorate the *Blut und Boden* mystique of Nazi ideology. But for the rest of the world, Schopenhauer is better known for his "pessimism" and caustic critiques of various aspects of European society. He is also regarded as a eccentric advocate of Buddhism.

Schopenhauer's position as a serious thinker was not helped by the fact that he was a clever writer. He became recognized through his critiques of the institutions of his time, not through his philosophical powers. Nevertheless, his concept of "Will" is far more important than his biting and humorous essays. It is also perhaps unfortunate that he used the word *Will* (*Der Wille*) to designate the force that he believed underlay all reality. His concept is exactly the same as that which modern physics has provided of the bundles of energy which compromise matter. However, Schopenhauer carried this concept to its logical conclusion and related it to the Kantian notion of the *noumenon*, the thing-in-itself lying behind all representations. *Will* refers to what lies behind inanimate as well as life forms, the difference between life and non-life lies merely in the complexity of the will. One needs to read and reread *The World as Will and Representation* to fully grasp the depth of thought which Schopenhauer brought to bear upon his subject. This is not an outmoded work, it is one that has not been sufficiently assimilated into the western world, especially the English-reading world. Fortunately, E.F.J. Payne has provided a remarkably good translation of Schopenhauer's most important writings.

Another circumstance that has worked against Schopenhauer's influence is the decline of *metaphysics* as a reputable mode of thought in contemporary society. The advances of technology and science have bewitched modern thinkers into believing that the phenomenal world has no need of metaphysics, that "scientific method," the method of objective observation, verification and systematization is the only reliable route to knowledge. There is an explicit devaluation of metaphysical conceptions, i.e. intuitive conceptions derived from personal experience, in favor of scientific models. The thinking human is compared to the model of a computer rather than the reality behind the senses, the brain and the instruments enlarging the purview of physiological systems.

Nevertheless, what Schopenhauer said in the nineteenth century is still true today, "Those who imagine crucibles and retorts to be the true and only source of all wisdom are in their way just as wrong as formerly were their antipodes, the scholastics. Thus just as the scholastics, involved entirely with their abstract concepts, struggled with these alone, neither knowing nor investigating anything besides them, so the scientists, involved entirely with their empiricism, accept nothing but what their eyes see, thinking with this one capacity to arrive at the ultimate ground of things . . ." A concept of metaphysics is necessary for everyone, even the crassest materialists. Karl Marx's metaphysics was the belief that a socialist system would produce happiness for human beings. Events have proven his belief to be inadequate. Contemporary scientists espousing monism hold the metaphysical concept that all reality is encompassed by a material world defined by instrumental observations and accessible to scientific methods of analysis. This is a metaphysical belief not founded upon scientific method. One might say it should be a hypothesis, subject to alteration. In fact, it is the outcome of the successes of technology, which has turned men's heads, so that the reality of spirit, i.e. the human will, is denied. Philosophers, who should have stood for something more than scientific monism, have largely become the apologists for its preeminence.

* * *

Schopenhauer is not popular among philosophers for two reasons. He ferociously attacked the institution of university philosophy to which virtually all "philosophers" belong and he unequivocally adopted a dualistic position in his own philosophy that is out of favor today. Schopenhauer asserted that the world consists of *Will*, the fundamental reality and *Phenomenon* (representation), the way in which reality experiences the outer world. Schopenhauer's monumental vision deserves more attention than it currently receives. There is no one in the twentieth century who has provided a vision of existence that equals Schopenhauer's in depth and breadth.

Within animate being, Schopenhauer conceived of will as essentially equivalent to will-to-live (inclusive of the will-to-procreate). This will is unconscious, pervasive and all—powerful in determining behavior. One may recognize this concept as the precursor to Freud's theories of the unconscious, the libido and the pleasure principle. In fact, Freud often mentioned Schopenhauer as a philosophical predecessor of psychoanalysis. However, Freud did not adopt Schopenhauer's dualism and psychoanalysis remained nominally as a form of scientific psychology.

Schopenhauer, however, in developing his ideas, took the fateful step of regarding conscious knowledge as something entirely distinct from the underlying will. Conscious knowledge, in his view, was something elaborated by the brain in the unconscious service of the will-to-live. He felt this "knowledge" was distinct in nature from the metaphysical will in that it was entirely a product of the workings of the brain. Here Schopenhauer fell into a contradiction that was noted by subsequent academics whom Schopenhauer had mercilessly castigated. If the physical brain was a phenomenon perceived by an observer, how could ideas and knowledge be a "phenomenon" of what was already a phenomenon? Schopenhauer could not have it both ways. Schopenhauer somewhere refers to a "will to knowledge" (*Erkenntniswollen*) implying the will is something more than the blind instinct to live. But generally, he is adamant in separating will from knowledge in their basic nature. Here too is the presentiment of Freudian theory.

In spite of his strenuous and repeated assertion of the subordination of knowledge to will, Schopenhauer finds "salvation" *Heilsordnung* to consist of emancipation of pure knowledge from the influence of the will. Here he enters into the realm of Buddhism, conceiving the human condition as capable of freeing itself from the tyranny of will. The concept of *Nirvana* is embraced which is the emancipation from desire, that is to say, from the dominance of the will.

All this is far removed from Schopenhauer's original intuition. If a living creature is fundamentally will and nothing more, and knowledge is only a creature of the will, how can knowledge suddenly take control of the destiny of the individual? In fact, Buddhism has no such glorified view of knowledge; liberation from desire is the result of a specific way of life prescribed by Buddhist traditions. In the case of Christianity, salvation is a matter of divine grace, something very different from the "mistress whore", knowledge. Schopenhauer's influence has suffered greatly through departure from his fundamental concept.

* * *

There is no reason to conceive of "will" in the original Schopenhauerian sense as a blind, limited, unchanging drive manifesting itself only the instinct to live, no different in a unicellular ameba than in a developed human being. The human insight into self discovers a will that is far more than that of the newborn infant. The developed will wants more than to live and procreate, it wants to know, to express itself, to penetrate the secrets of the logos. The more it enters into the knowledge of being, the more it expresses this knowledge—and expression is the consolidation of knowledge—the more it yearns to enter more deeply into the labyrinth. The concept that man is a metaphysical animal, dating back to the Greeks, acknowledges the existence of a will to know in human beings. Knowing is a transforming experience, one who looks into the nature of being, especially human being, is a transformed person whose will manifests this transformation. To be "spiritual" means to be one who has gazed deeply into the nature of things and has assimilated the knowledge that is forthcoming from this gaze. Deeply moving experiences obtained in exceptional circumstances may provide such knowledge. A person may emerge from a war experience, from an intense relationship, from extreme danger or exertion as a changed being as a consequence of the knowledge provided by these experiences. More often it is the cumulative weight of more modest daily experience and contact with the minds of others which results in a changed interior state transcending the simple "will to live" and representing its deepened metaphysical state.

"Knowledge" derived from exceptional events, relationships and learning is to be distinguished from information acquisition that serves to solidify one's own position in the material world. This type of knowledge is what Schopenhauer and Freud had in mind when they refer to knowledge in the service of the will-to-live or id. The explosion of information occurring in the computer era represents the unrestrained materialism of our times serving only the will to live." Knowledge is Power" is the epigraph deserving of placement on every computer screen providing information to its user. Knowledge that is utilitarian for material purposes is identifiable by the motive for its acquisition. If knowledge is acquired *in order* that the tasks of daily living are more readily accomplished, *in order* to improve one's financial condition, *in order* to enhance power and prestige, *in order* to improve health and material welfare, *in order* to amuse and otherwise divert the individual—all this is knowledge gained for ulterior purposes. The language is not adequate; one must constantly distinguish between informational knowledge and transformational knowledge. The former refers to Freudian knowledge in the service of the will to live (i.e. pleasure principle), the latter to the transfiguration of the will consequent to this knowledge. A great mystery is the fact that knowledge transformational for one person is only informational for another. It can never be forgotten that the mind of the knower is as significant as the content of what is known.

* * *

Kant's modesty permitted him to perceive that the "thing-in-itself" (*ding-an-sich*), which following Schopenhauer's lead may be termed "will", cannot be known by *Homo sapiens* in the same way as he knows the phenomenal world. To call something "will" or "force" gives it a name but does not give insight into its essential state. Our minds are not equipped by nature to comprehend the thing-in-itself. The hubris that ignores this perception leads to breakdown of the human psyche. We can only perceive its effects or, in the case of our own selves, gaze into our own personalities. Even this introspection, conducted as it is by the analytic mind, has limited value in understanding our essential nature. The human mind does not have the capacity for full insight into the interior world of will. But we can apprehend the effects of changes of the will, more clearly in ourselves, more by analogy in others. Thus one can discern the move to a more metaphysical state when the will is oriented to transformational knowledge as contrasted with the other type.

One of Goethe's letters to Schiller, quoted by Nietzsche in his essay *Use and Abuse of History*, contains the statement: "I hate everything that merely instructs me without increasing or directly quickening my activity." Now we must go beyond Goethe and say "I hate everything that merely instructs me without transfiguring my will." There may be an element of hyperbole in this modification but in this most unmetaphysical of times, this era of purely technologically directed activity, some hyperbole is in order to save the spirit. If one accepts "will" as the embodiment of metaphysical man, then we may truly say that which does not transform the will is to be despised. The authenticity of this transfiguration is to be contrasted to the false metaphysics of the profit-oriented world. As Schopenhauer has said, the only obligation of metaphysics is to be true (*wahr*). Other obligations such as being happy, optimistic, theistic, moral, socially supportive, etc. must give way to its primary obligation of authenticity.

Schopenhauer does not elaborate on the meaning of the word *wahr* in his discussions on the subject. Authenticity or truth has been a concern of profound thinkers from Heraclitus to Heidegger. Philosophers conceive of truth in its antique Greek meaning of *aletheia*, the unveiling of reality. Kierkegaard announced that truth is subjectivity, emphasizing the connection of truth to the human condition. Nietzsche independently recapitulated Kierkegaard's concept minus its connection to Kierkegaard's Christian commitment Heidegger has discussed the concept of truth at length from an etymological point of view although characteristically avoids a clarifying statement. These conceptions of truth are far removed from the *scientific* truth that is a matter of empirical observation and verification. Scientific truth deals only with phenomenal reality, philosophical truth with all of reality. Where this distinction is not clearly respected, there will never be a real understanding of the meaning of the word truth. The ultimate expression of commitment to philosophical truth is to be found in St. John's version of Jesus' encounter with Pilate where the former asserted he was born to bear witness to the truth. His own subjectivity was the truth for Jesus. Pilate, as is well known, expressed his uncertainty about this idea, a comment that Nietzsche later found to be the only tolerable statement in the entire New Testament!

* * *

It has been said that the errors of great men are more fruitful than the truisms of mediocre ones. This is nowhere more correct than in the case of Schopenhauer who was led into many errors by his angry nature and his reactions against the philosophical establishment of his day. He was also coarse, dogmatic and intolerant in many of his judgments, even by nineteenth century German standards. Yet he is to be revered because he held to a standard of devotion to authenticity–truth–which left the German philosophical establishment struggling in the rear. One does not have to share his contempt of Hegel, Fichte and Schelling to find that he was infinitely superior to them in quality of thought and clarity of exposition. Far more than Schopenhauer or Nietzsche, it was the glorification of race and state by Fichte and Hegel that were the antecedents to the catastrophic militarism and racial doctrines of Germany in the first half of the twentieth century.

Schopenhauer fulfilled the dictum of Bergson that any philosopher worthy of the name has never said more than a single thing. The single thing that he said and defended in thousands of pages over a forty year writing career was that the will was the thing-in-itself behind the variegated world of phenomena. He defined this will metaphysically, thus earning for himself the disdain and disinterest of the scientific monists who dominate our culture today. But the underlying truth is that a human is an *animal metaphysicum* with metaphysical needs who will be never satisfied by a purely physical conception of the universe. Schopenhauer spoke to these needs without recourse to superannuated, institutionalized religions or reliance upon any type of occultism or revelationism. He relied solely upon the mind that is a possession of all members of the species *Homo sapiens*. We may not accept all his conclusions and may develop his ideas in new directions but he is the great pioneer of modern metaphysical thought in the western world.

* * *

Today we live in a world that has persuaded itself the soul does not exist. Our entire way of life, our devotion to the machine culture, our mania for material acquisition, our craze for information and stimulation from external sources, our love affair with instruments, all these lead away from awareness–not to speak of reverence–of the soul. Those who have been successful in the contest for wealth pander to the acquisition mania in the most disgraceful manner; those who have lost out squander their limited resources on lotteries and gambling. The metaphysical need of humans is blocked by devotion to technology. The antique Greeks thought it was impossible to have many possessions and still lead the life of *arete*, excellence. Within the purist Cynic movement (not to be confused with the modern meaning of the term), it was required that one's possessions be strictly limited. A similar attitude was held by the early Christian communities, we know what Jesus thought of riches—one's heart where was one's treasure. Our treasures are internal combustion vehicles, entertainment machines, land and property, bank accounts and stock portfolios. Nothing today can compete with these things and their like–no one has an image of the treasures of the soul.

There are many conceptions of treasures of the soul. Family attachments, for example, are biologically based values. Preservation of and sacrifice for children or other blood relationships are a manifestation of the will to live which is the most primitive of spiritual attainments. Sociobiologists in our time talk of preservation of gene pools–it appears that altruistic behavior is merely a more sophisticated version of the will to live inherent in all things. But it is in reverence for the spiritual nature of the self that true spirituality lies. Perhaps this extends to spiritual relationships with others although, as Kierkegaard suggested, it is debatable whether such relationships can ever really exist in the world of objects. One's own relationship to the eternal is the essential manifestation of spirituality. Whose spirit does not resonate with this last statement has lost the connection to his own soul.

In spite of the overwhelming materialist orientation of western society, the western man still demonstrates a will to know more than the mechanics of utilitarian technology. The yearning for spiritual fulfillment is to be found everywhere. Consequently, as is to be expected in a market oriented culture such as exists in America, there has appeared a lively spirituality industry purporting to cater to those needful of spiritual fulfillment beyond the traditional religions for children. Bookstore shelves are filled with small and large volumes purporting to minister to the needs of those in need of "spirit." For the most part, these can be divided into two categories; one–those which follow the well-developed "how to" tradition of American culture, how to increase spiritual awareness and two—those which are cast in a scholarly format, reviewing and summarizing the concepts of spirituality which have achieved notoriety. The first follow the method of the inspirational teacher, the second that of the analytical scholar. In both cases, consideration of the market is often paramount, the writings must *sell* in order for them to be cast in book form.

The contradiction in this approach lies in the fact that spirituality and marketability are two very different phenomena. Expansion of the metaphysical mind–the soul–is not acquired through "how to" techniques or through the labyrinths of scholarly study. These methods denature the mind and do not lead to spiritual development. Christianity has learned through centuries of experience that an internal turning or rebirth is needful for such development to occur. Institutional Christianity attributes this turning to God's "grace," the intervention of a holy spirit into the human soul but this is a sophism, explaining nothing of the nature of this event. I am inclined to believe that every human being possesses a drive toward spirituality which is always impeded, to a lesser or greater degree, by his society and culture. It is not grace as an addition from without which is necessary, it is grace as an unlearning, an emancipation from the orientation toward the concrete imposed by one's material milieu. No experience, cultural or otherwise, which does not provide a powerful redirection of one's life will be of any lasting value.

* * *

Great spiritual teachers are people who project their inner selves into their work and whose lives, in some way, express their individuality. They are not the professionals of society, they are not priests, pastors, professors or psychologists, they are people who "write with their blood" as Nietzsche has said, who have something to say transcending the conventions of the time. They are the "fanatics of the mind" who know the difference between the inner and the outer self. In this category fall Schopenhauer, Kierkegaard, Max Stirner, Nicolai Berdyaev and, of course, Nietzsche himself. Decidedly not in this category are Einstein, Lenin, Hitler or Mother Theresa. These former types are rarely recognized in their lifetime or even posthumously by society and we should assume that the greatest souls die unknown and unrecognized. This is no loss to them but is a tragic loss to their society which needed their influence. Today, in the United States, it would be impossible for the types mentioned above to be heard, thus we are limited to the outpouring of those who can make a profit for the culture industry. One recourse to this state of affairs is the descent into violent madness such as the phenomenon of an individual achieving notoriety through mailing letter bombs to prominent individuals.

The key to the illness of our era lies in understanding the lure of the products of technology. Why is it that our world is so in love with mechanical devices? Why is it that people will beat a path to the door of the one who devises a better mousetrap?–or a more entertaining spectacle?–or a sleeker contraption to carry one from one place to another or any of the myriad of products that appeal to consumers everywhere? It is certainly evident that all these products enormously complicate the lives of their users. Stress levels are higher, work is more demanding, time more and more is at a premium. The only apparent gainers are the captains of technology who reap gigantic profits from the consumer mania fostered upon society—if they can really said to be gainers. Why do people want so many things to which they become quickly habituated and which serve mainly to increase the burdens of daily life?

Many answers have been offered to this question–the lure of novelty, the appeal of "conspicuous consumption," the sheer pleasure of possession, the desire for new experiences . . . I would like to state my own conviction that the underlying force driving the consumerism of society is a negative one, a universal repressive neurosis which seeks to escape the *metaphysical need* of *Homo sapiens*. People fear true leisure and the contemplative insights associated with it; they will literally do anything that will relieve them of the necessity to lead an interior life. They fear their own soul and repress all activity associated it. That is why modern science that denies existence of the soul is so joyfully welcomed by the materialists of the world. It is not profit or power that principally drives the society, these are derivative phenomena, it is rather the unconscious fear of looking within oneself. Consequently the scientist is looked upon as the savior of the world and the philosopher (not the professor of philosophy) is an object of scorn and derision.

However, the metaphysical need of humans is not abolished by scorning it. It lies in quiet wait, raising its head at unexpected times and producing the most unlikely effects at unpredictable moments. Thus the addict of technology cannot rid himself of a yearning for some form of metaphysical fulfillment and will often participate in the most childlike programs that cater to this need. The problem of death looms large in the mind of one without a metaphysical concept of its meaning; the most powerful or wealthiest individual will engage in the most ridiculous behavior to prolong a life made useless by age or disease. Pharaonic monuments are planned which somehow are expected to perpetuate the presence of the extinguished life. Refusal to face the metaphysical problem of existence with all one's heart and mind will come back to haunt the individual. Yet in the flower of their lives, individuals for the sake of money, power, prestige or material accomplishment will, as Nietzsche perceptively observed, "give away their souls in order not to be troubled by them."

The one addicted to material world consoles himself with the thought that his addiction has to do with what is *real* while the world of reflection is composed of what is not real, of illusions. He has no confidence in what he cannot touch, see and hear or what does not give him a direct experience of and power over the world of nature. The professionals of philosophy fall into the vernacular of the materialists, accepting the belief that science and reality are one. Thus the modern philistine (devotee of technology) deludes himself that he is participating in "real" life and misses its essential purpose for human beings, the development of metaphysical consciousness. The scientific spirit is of no use here because it is merely a method of dealing with one aspect of organized life, the part that has to do with mastery over nature. This aspect is becoming less and less significant for human life since nature is all but fully mastered. Observation, verification and construction are tools useful in overcoming the perils or limitations of individual life but no good at all in matters of the spirit.

The materialist when confronted with the metaphysical substance of the mind thinks to himself, "What is all this nonsense? None of this can be proven. None of it is real, none of it is worth anything for getting on in life." Thus he misses the essential reality of intelligent being which has to do with *enlightenment*–a metaphysical concept–about the underlying nature of reality. Enlightenment is not reached through proof, it is a matter of spiritual assimilation. One's perspective determines how assimilation occurs. The creation of a spiritual being depends upon the perspective of that being. Rather than truth or falsehood, one needs to develop the concepts of inferior and superior. Certain forms of enlightenment are superior to others. Goethe was superior to Hegel, Nietzsche was superior to Hitler. There is no one who is more susceptible to inferior forms of enlightenment than are the materialists of the world who have neglected their interior selves. Perhaps it is a matter of capacity, metaphysical matters require more intelligence and judgement than scientific ones since there are no formulas or techniques to rely upon for verification of value. There is only the intuition of the developed mind founded upon experience, understanding and that mysterious quality which Christians have referred to divine grace.

The materialist way of life is essentially a form of animal life, fortified by invention, memory and abstract reasoning. Ten fingers and frontal lobes play the principal part in human superiority over other animals. But the materialist worldview, no matter how highly developed, is in no essential way different from the goals and methods of other animals. It is in the soul, the metaphysical domain, where humans exhibit the significant advance over other forms of life. Therefore, it is in this area of attention to the metaphysical that one's energies need to be focussed if one is to be fulfilled as a human being.

* * *

For two millennia the institution of Christianity has been the vehicle for the encouragement of metaphysical thought in western society. Unlike the eastern mode of spirituality, it has evolved a highly organized church, a defined holy scripture and a doctrine enumerating the necessary beliefs required of pious Christians– the trinity, the virgin birth and the resurrection of Christ. Upon the platform of these dogmas there has developed a spiritual sense largely preempting other forms of spirituality. Eastern ways of thought have recently gained some foothold in western society but these are tenuous, depending largely on alienated intellectuals, especially Jewish ones, for their influence. Judaism persists in an astonishing manner as it has for far longer than Christianity; it is now a tiny minority in the Euro-American world, destined apparently to finally assimilate within the larger Christian society.

Christianity has been the traditional means by which metaphysical consciousness evolved in Europe and the Americas. Traditions are always a mixed blessing; they are the source of much good and much evil for the individual. They are a source of strength and satisfaction but they are also a straitjacket. Christianity is the metaphysical straitjacket of western culture. In order to access the spiritual insights of two thousand years of Christian experience, one must bow to the childish doctrines of the churches. In the metaphysical domain more than anywhere else, one must purify belief with the cleansing acid of an intellectual conscience, a *skepsis* that is part of the intellectual heritage of the Greco-Roman world. Without this *skepsis*, one is at the mercy of all the vagaries of human desires, illusions and falsifications. To accept Christian dogmas is to suspend one's mind in the very area where the mind must be most active–the formulation of the principal problem of personal existence and the discovery of its meaning to the extent possible for a finite human. These problems and discoveries cannot be delegated to doctors of churches or to holy scriptures no matter how clothed with tradition they may be. The outcome of faith prior to understanding is a stunted mind and a fanatical personality.

Children are the ones who are subjected to the worst dangers from religious indoctrination Schopenhauer expressed his view that a child subjected to religious training prior to the age of eight years could never be wholly independent in the arena of metaphysical thought. Rather bind a child's head with wrappings to regulate its shape than fill it with the untruths of institutionalized religious doctrines.

Every child deserves the right to develop his mind to the extent possible for him. He or she needs to be prepared to one day cope with the ultimate questions: What am I? Why am I here? What must I do? Where am I going? This preparation is every bit as important as training for a trade or career which will support his material existence. Molding the mind according to dogmatic religious belief at critical stages of development will damage it forever. I suspect it was this insight which was responsible for Schopenhauer's contempt and Nietzsche's rage toward established Christianity. Every right-thinking person *should* be contemptuous and enraged about a system of education which ignores or impedes the development of the capacity to independently seek out metaphysical truth.

Schopenhauer, like Goethe and Emerson, was more accepting of Christianity than was Nietzsche. For some reason, he preferred to vent his rage on Judaism rather than Christianity. It is he who coined the phrase, "religion is the metaphysics of the masses." It is of course this concept which has fortified the Roman Catholic hierarchy to perpetuate itself according to the model inherited from the Roman Empire. Unamuno dramatized the problem of the Catholic priest with an intellectual conscience in his novel *San Manuel Bueno, martir*. Dostoevski was less charitable than Unamuno, he likened the Grand Inquisitor, the historical emblem of Roman Catholic authority to Antichrist (*The Brothers Karamazov*). These issues need to be brought back to current culture and not buried in the dustheaps of academic studies. The concept of metaphysics for the masses should be once and for all abandoned if democracy has any real meaning–better no metaphysics at all than a solidified doctrinal cast stultifying the mind and rendering it incapable of genuine spirituality.

When one rejects the "metaphysics of the masses," one has a responsibility to identify a "better" metaphysics that truly answers the human metaphysical need. Nietzsche attempted to do this in his essay entitled *Schopenhauer as Educator*. Here he elaborates his idea that nature strives to develop superior persons, even often at the expense of humanity as a whole. Nietzsche proposed three types of individuals representative of superior persons; the philosopher, the artist and the saint (note no politicians or generals). He suggested that the development of these types is the fundamental idea of culture; not only as separate persons but as a potential within every individual who aspires to a higher form of being. No doubt this is a Utopian idea of culture, it presupposes the *values* that would make such an orientation possible. Later Nietzsche epitomized his concept with his famous assertion "Die vornehme Seele hat Ehrfurcht vor sich." (The noble soul has reverence for itself.)

If the future of the human race lies in the fulfillment of the human race as *Homo sapiens*, then Nietzsche is the great precursor figure of this destiny. However, this is a most uncertain possibility, nothing since the creative period of Nietzsche's life indicates that the values exist which would make this future possible.

* * *

Ultimately, we members of a peculiar species must conceive of ourselves as creatures who are created in order to *think*. Science carries us along this path for a certain distance but it limits us to thought concerned with material existence. Beyond material existence, there is the realm of thought itself that must be confronted. Here we enter into a totally new level of being, something requiring a new state of mind. No matter how far we go, there is no end to the human mind—a situation recognized by Heraclitus at the dawn of thought. But as long as one uses material being as a model, this realm cannot be entered. One is then shackled to material existence.

"To have existed as a thinking being has profound meaning"– this is the answer to the death which nature imposes on every living thing. The human individual exists in the annals of time; the significance of this existence has to with the thoughts his mind created, all else, as Thoreau said, is merely a record of the winds that blew while he was here. Not in the memory of mankind but in the reality of being lies the significance of human existence with its thoughts.

In my essay, *Souls Exist*, I considered Augustine's statement that there were only two questions worthy of note, God and the soul. I reduced this short list even further–only the soul deserved consideration. My conviction has grown since then that there is nothing to gain and everything to lose by ruminating on the unknowable idea of God. It is reverence for one's own soul–however, this entity is conceived–which is essential, the more one reveres a God, the less he reveres his soul. The idea that belief in God is the individual's "charter of liberty" providing freedom from the tyrannical forces of society is merely exchanging one tyranny for another. One needs the courage to exist for oneself, without the guiding strings of a theology derived from the minds of others. An unknown nature endows us with a will-to-live, it is this will within us which naturally transforms itself into a will-to-know requiring nothing more than our own natural faculties. If there is a superior force dwelling somewhere, it is not given to human beings to have knowledge of its nature.

A poetical impulse is required for saying certain things:

> My poem is a psalm to my created self,
> I am the single Me, the only truth I know,
> I am the mission, the sacred task,
> quietly I consider myself,
> I have a strange beauty!

I have made the vow of freedom,
the vow never to be broken,
again, I set free the mystic vessel of my life,
again, the restraining moorings are released,
vigilantly, watching the treacherous reefs,
I move toward the open sea,
I make my way to deep waters,
my spirit calmly scanning the distant horizon,
searching for an unseen destination.

extract from The Last Transport in *Philosophical Artwork*

* * *

FINIS

Printed in the United States
5302